D1275288

Creative Techniques

Creative Techniques

for Stylish Cards, Tags, Boxes, and more

LESLIE CAROLA

Creative Consultant:
Judy Ritchie

Arena Books Associates, LLC

www.arenabooksassociates.com
ISBN: 978-0-9797922-5-0
This edition of Creative Techniques for Cards, Tags, Boxes, and More
has been prepared for Crafters Choice Book Club.

An Arena Books Associates, LLC book

Project Director: Leslie Carola
Creative Consultant: Judy Ritchie
Design: Elizabeth Johnsboen
Photography: Jon Van Gorder Studio, Inc.

Projects: Judy Ritchie (www.greatamericanstampstore.com)
Susan Swan (www.susanswan.com)
Irene Seifer (www.greatamericanstampstore.com)
Janet Williams, Robert Carola, Anastasia Bosakowski, Leslie Carola
Projects are credited to designers on page.

Special papers: Peach/green floral, Asian floral, Blue vine copyright 2012 by Alexis Seabrook
(www.alexisseabrook.com).

Printed in China

CONTENTS

Introduction

Paper is an extraordinary material. It is readily available, usually inexpensive, easy to store, and almost irresistible. How often do we reach to smooth a ruffled sheet, explore the texture of handmade paper, or just stroke the surface of another? For paper crafters, it is a sensual, inviting canvas that responds to the touch. We can tear, cut, bend, fold, layer, and color paper. We can attach paper to another substance—like glass, acrylic, wood, or board—or add other materials to a paper surface. Whether we choose to alter the paper itself by cutting or folding it or simply add color or affix an element to its surface, we can succesfully, even magically, transform a simple slip of paper into distinctive artwork. The process is creative, engaging, and fun.

More than seventy projects are included in *Creative Techniques for Cards, Tags, Boxes, and More,* arranged into four chapters by technique—stamping, folding, cutting, and special effects. We offer dozens of ways to create imaginative cards, tags, boxes, bags, ornaments, and table-top items. None of the techniques is difficult. Some of the projects are quick and easy, others demand a bit more time and attention. Many of the projects could be in one or another section because they employ several techniques or materials.

This book is a compilation, a sampling really, of some of the best projects from a few earlier books—*Cut It, Fold It, Use It; Year-Round Paper Crafts; Great Cards and Tags*—plus many new projects. In fact, almost half of the projects are new, updated using new materials and designs that have become available from craft suppliers. We have included some step-by-step, how-to instructions for some projects, others we have simply pointed attention to the palette, the shapes, or the composition. We have also included a few templates to help in the construction of some projects. Look through the book, get ideas, and create the projects your own way. Use your imagination. Explore and experiment.

Gathering some fundamentals of design before starting to make your own projects will help you to develop your creative intuition. Learn to trust your own eye to tell you what does or doesn't work. The rules for designing are few: create a strong focal point with pleasing color, texture, and balance. One of the design elements we are most interested in is the space left around an image. The shape of the created image is the positive shape. The space left around the created image is the negative space. It spotlights the main attraction. Please don't feel compelled to fill every space on a card, tag, or any other project. Think of the action in a stage production. Isolate the main attraction and arrange the supporting characters in a pleasing or dramatic way. Present your design "onstage" by making sure the focal point is showcased with breathing room.

Another favorite technique of ours is lifting an image off a mat or part of an image off the paper, using foam tape or dots. This technique is frequently referred to as "popping." A simple stamped image is an easy project, but you can extend the effect by embellishing with extra color, layers of mats, text, or special adornments. Adding layers of colorful mats behind a component or lifting an element off the page adds dimension to the composition and draws our attention directly to the featured element, the

focal point. Creating a balanced composition is a helpful tip for crafters starting out. A composition can be centered and symmetric, or off-center and asymmetric, or it could be a symmetric arrangement placed off-center. Details make a difference. Look for surprises as you work. Much more than the sum of its parts, a well-crafted project is a work of art.

We respond to color emotionally. Warm colors are exciting, stimulating. Cool colors are calming. When choosing a palette for a project, think of a favorite bouquet of flowers and select from those tones. Or you can work with a color wheel (at right) if you would be more comfortable that way. The point is to be creative and have fun.

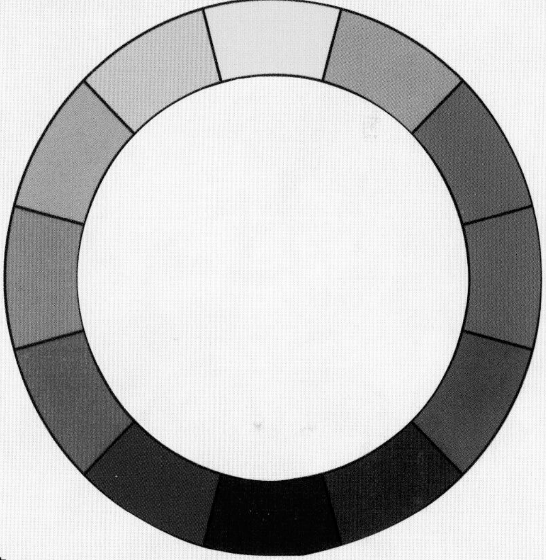

You don't need a lot of materials to start, but you will probably find yourself gathering and saving materials and tools for future projects. As you do so it would be wise to plan where and how you will store these items. An organized work space is helpful. Before starting to work on a project gather all the necessary supplies at hand. It is frustrating to have to stop to locate a tool or material in order to complete a project.

We've heard several of the contributing crafters refer to "playing with the material." That is our hope—that you play with color, play with shapes, play with the composition. See the possibilities and be open to surprises. Don't be afraid to mix and match. Crafting is a dynamic and fun part of our lives. Celebrate life—moments large and small— with your crafting.

STAMPING

Rubber stamping is easy, effective, and fun. And the results can be artistic, elegant, whimsical, or playful. The techniques in this chapter are not difficult to master; some are very simple, others might seem complicated but usually involve only the addition of an extra element—a ribbon, flower, stitching, or even a Zentangle doodle. Small finishing touches, or embellishments, like the ones in this chapter, add striking texture and detail, transforming simple stamped images to elegant finished projects.

One thing to consider before starting to stamp is the ink you will use. There are many varieties of inks now available. Knowing what each one is meant

for will help prevent any mishaps with ink that dried too quickly or not at all! **Dye ink** is transparent, dries quickly on paper surfaces, and works well on glossy coated paper, matte coated, or uncoated cardstock. **Pigment ink** is opaque, slow to dry, and leaves a crisp, clear color. You would use pigment ink when embossing an image because the stamped image needs to stay wet long enough to accept the embossing powder. **Chalk ink pads** are a hybrid between dye and pigment inks: they are quick drying (like dye ink) and the soft chalk finish is opaque (like pigment ink). **Opalite inks** produce a pearl-like finish. **Alcohol inks** are effective for nonporous surfaces like glass or plastic, or even highly glossy coated paper. The many different kinds of inks allow you to create endless variations.

Karen Lockhart

Coloring with Pencils

Karen Lockhart takes the art of the craft of stamping up a notch with her beautifully designed stamps and colored-pencil treatment. And she isn't afraid to add a touch of whimsy. The classic card is enhanced simply with layers of soft shaded Prismacolor™ pencil, colored like perfectly ripe pears with highlights and shading. The tag offers one pear with intriguing designs—sometimes called Zentangle—drawn with black line on the colored image.

NOTE: The projects from Karen Lockhart on these first two spreads are similar in composition. Their elegant simplicity makes it easy to create your own projects in a similar style.

Different materials accept color differently. Colored pencils work best on paper with a little "tooth" or texture—a paper like cardstock. Choose a colored pencil with a thick soft core of high quality pigments to help blend and shade color for a luxurious burnished effect. In this project, contrasting light and dark highlights embellish the edges and centers of the leaves of the artichoke. The patterned mat behind the black mat balances the texture of the artichoke itself. The solid black mat provides a definite ground for the silhouetted image.

Karen Lockhart

CREATING THE PROJECT

1. Stamp the artichoke image in black ink on slightly "toothy" white cardstock.
2. Build layers of color with several shades of green and highlight the tips of the leaves and the thick stalk with a soft purple. (Doodle some flower-like repetitive swirls on the tag with a fine black marker and highlight the drawing with purple.)
3. Silhouette the colored artichoke.
4. "Pop" the silhouetted artichoke off the black mat on the tag with several small pieces of foam tape. Adhere the sihouetted artichoke flat onto the black mat on the card.
5. For the card, layer a panel of tiny gingham-printed paper on a slightly larger square of purple cardstock. Adhere the central image (the artichoke) on a black mat. Reverse the matting for the tag: Layer the black mat on a slightly larger purple mat before layering on a gingham mat and then the tag.
6. Accent the outer edge of the gingham mat of the card, and around the black mat on the tag, with glitter glue. Add text if you wish. Punch a hole in the top left corner and loop a decorative ribbon through the punchef hole.

Karen Lockhart

There are many ways to add color to stamped images. Colored pencil is a favorite choice for many crafters wanting to add subtle shading. To vary the texture change the pressure you put on the pencil as you gently rub in layers of color. Evenly pressured side-to-side strokes create a smooth layer of pigment to build on. Increase pressure as you stroke to add shadowy texture. Keep your colored pencils sharp and clean for optimum use. We recommend that you keep a pencil sharpener handy as you work. Peas decorated with black Zentangle doodling whimsically enlivens the silhouetted popped pea pod on the tag.

Karen Lockhart

Color captures our attention immediately. These three little mushrooms look like they've just stepped out of a Walt Disney chorus line. You look at them and smile—the colorful palette, the almost-swaying stances, and the cheerful decorative touches (Zentangle doodles on the tag and drops of Liquid Pearls™ on the card) are hard to resist. All is accomplished with layers of colored-pencil strokes, layers of mats, and a few embellishments. Layers of alternating color-coordinated patterned and solid mats draw our eyes directly to the focal point. Imaginative, charming, fun, and not difficult.

Coloring with Inks

A leafless winter tree stamped in brown ink on ivory cardstock is a canvas on which you can add details appropriate to the season. Here, twenty-five tiny red hearts and twenty-five tiny (almost not visible) pink hearts are stamped onto the bare brown tree branches. The layered mats draw our attention directly to the off-center tree—the focal point—while adding texture. An interesting design tip: the tree is centered on its mat, but the mat is shifted off-center for an asymmetric arrangement. The translucent white paper is hand-stamped with a fern patttern, contributing to the soft texture. The small text box with a dark border, lower right, visually balances the larger, but lighter, off-center focal point.

Judy Ritchie

Creating the Project

1. Stamp the tree in brown pigment ink on ivory cardstock.
2. Stamp twenty-five tiny pink hearts and twenty-five tiny red hearts like leaves along the branches of the trees.
3. Trim and layer the stamped panel on a pink mat.
4. Stamp small white ferns randomly on white vellum to create an interesting pattern. Layer the stamped vellum onto a red horizontally folded card.
5. Stamp a greeting on ivory cardstock, trim, insert in a small dark frame.
6. Adhere the panels as shown.

A dark solid image stamped in Pearlescent Chocolate Tsukineko Brilliance pigment ink over Sea Breeze, Tea Leaves, and Turquoise Gem VersaMagic foliage and flourish produces an eye-catching composition in an engaging palette. The solid stamp demands no extra color, just what is used for the stamped images themselves. Stamp the branches, flowers, and flourish first, let dry, and then stamp the bird. Layer a generous length of double-sided ribbon under the brown and blue mats before adhering to the card/folio. Tie a bow at the right.

Irene Seifer

Irene Seifer

Chalk inks produce a lovely soft opaque finish. A monochromatic color scheme conveys a feeling of harmony and calm. This simple palette of several tones of green offers an appealing note. The dark-green tree stands in front of a free-hand chalked background on a white cardstock panel. Stamp the tree first in Brilliance Pearlescent Ivy and then add the Pebbles Metallic Cream chalk using the small cotton balls and alligator clip that come with the chalks. Dab on a small amount of chalk ink with a light touch; tap off any excess. A narrow dark-green mat supports the central image. One printed (Washi paper from Hanko) and one solid green paper form the background. A column of gold Asian calligraphic sticker characters look like a signature.

Judy Ritchie

Judy Ritchie

Repeated stamp images can be arranged in different patterns to create very different looks. A small stamp can be used ingeniously in several ways. For one card, above right, this small flower image is stamped in red and the leaves in green multiple times to form the shape of a large heart. For another card, above left, the same image is stamped several times in purple and green and arranged as a bouquet in a vase, and then the bloom alone is stamped to embellish the center of a row of punched white flowers along the bottom of the decorative paper mat. Remember that crafting is about celebrating life and having fun. Use the stamps as an extended canvas for your creativity.

Judy Ritchie

A solid single bloom (no added coloring needed) sitting in an outline wheelbarrow is stamped with Memento pigment inks on white card-stock. Apply the ink directly to the stamp to create this multicolor image. Color the wheel-barrow interior with a Copic marker in light brown. Trim the stamped panel and layer on a hot-pink mat, and then adhere this to a large earth-toned striped paper mounted on a white card. Attach a word panel below the stamped image with hot-pink brads that visually connect the text panel to the main image and add a textural touch to the card. Clean, simple, and effective.

A composition similar to the one above is offered here with a lighter palette—extending the pink and white tones. The coloring on the pink flower and green stem and leaves as well as the blue border on the white cardstock panel is done with Copic markers, the highest quality marker available, made in Japan by the Too Corporation. The softness of the project is extended with a wavy-edged punched gray cardstock mat and a large mat of tiny pink and white polka dot. A green ribbon wrapped near the bottom, ties it all together.

Judy Ritchie

The lovely effect of white flowers on a colored background is created easily with this stamp. The stamp is unusual: the flower images are carved into the rubber mat, making them recessed and therefore drop out of the background color. Most stamps are created the other way around, with the image raised and the background recessed so that the image is inked and the background is not. Small glass flowers embellish the flower centers. An informal yellow ribbon wraps around the matted image before it is attached to the card.

Judy Ritchie

CREATING THE PROJECT

1. Color the stamp with dye ink, applying the ink to the stamp bed carefully.

2. Stamp the image on white cardstock. Trim the cardstock panel to 3 by 3 ½ inches, the size of the stamped image.

3. Adhere the panel to a purple mat leaving a ⅛-inch border around the stamped panel.

4. Add glass beads to the flower centers.

Judy Ritchie

A simple composition in a pleasing, soft palette is eye-catching. A successful recipe for creating a pleasing project often includes a centered composition on layers of mats. In this case the image is centered horizontally and just above center vertically. The background paper is a strong colorful print so one violet mat to support the dominant color of the stamped image is enough to cleanly present the focal point of the project—the lovely violets. A drop of Orchid Liquid Pearls enhances the center of each of the three stamped violets. A strip of green striped Trendy Tape grounds the image at the bottom of the stamped panel.

CREATING THE PROJECT

1. Stamp the violets with Memento black ink on white cardstock.
2. Color both the flowers and stems with Copic markers — two shades of violet for the flowers (the centers of the flowers are a little darker than the petals) and green for the stems and leaves.
3. Add a drop of Orchid Liquid Pearls to the center of each stamped flower.
4. Cut the stamped cardstock panel to a 2 ½-inch square.
5. Cut a 2 ½-inch strip of green striped Trendy Tape, and place it along the bottom edge of the stamped cardstock panel so that the top stripe is just above the base of the flower image.
6. Adhere to a 2 ¾-inch square violet mat. Layer on the printed paper background cut to leave ⅛-inch border to the 4 ¼ by 5 ½-inch white card.

Judy Ritchie

Coloring with Copic Markers

Copic markers color cleanly with permanent, non-toxic, alcohol-based dye ink that dries acid free. Alcohol inks will bleed through most paper stocks so, for best results, layer the colored pictures onto other paper stock. Since Copic markers are alcohol based, use Memento or VersaFine inks to stamp the image on clean white or ivory cardstock. Watercolor paper is too absorbent for good results. For clean, smooth areas, color slowly in circles with the side of your brush to really saturate the paper. To avoid streaking make sure all your edges stay "wet." If you have a very large area, color it in first with the blender marker and, while the paper is still damp, work with your color marker over the top.

CREATING THE PROJECT

1. Stamp the image with Memento Grey Flannel ink on white cardstock. Let the ink dry completely before adding color. Create a base coat of the areas to be colored with an even covering of the lightest of your selected colors.

2. Add shading with a darker color in the same color family.

3. Blend the colors by recoloring the sections where the two colors meet with the lighter color. Cut the stamped panel to 4 ⅞ by 3 ⅜ inches. Cut the brown and white polka dot mat to 6 by 4 ¼ inches; layer it on the white card.

4. Cut the pink cardstock mat to 5 ⅛ by 3 ⅝ inches. Layer the stamped panel on the pink mat and adhere this to the polka dot mat.

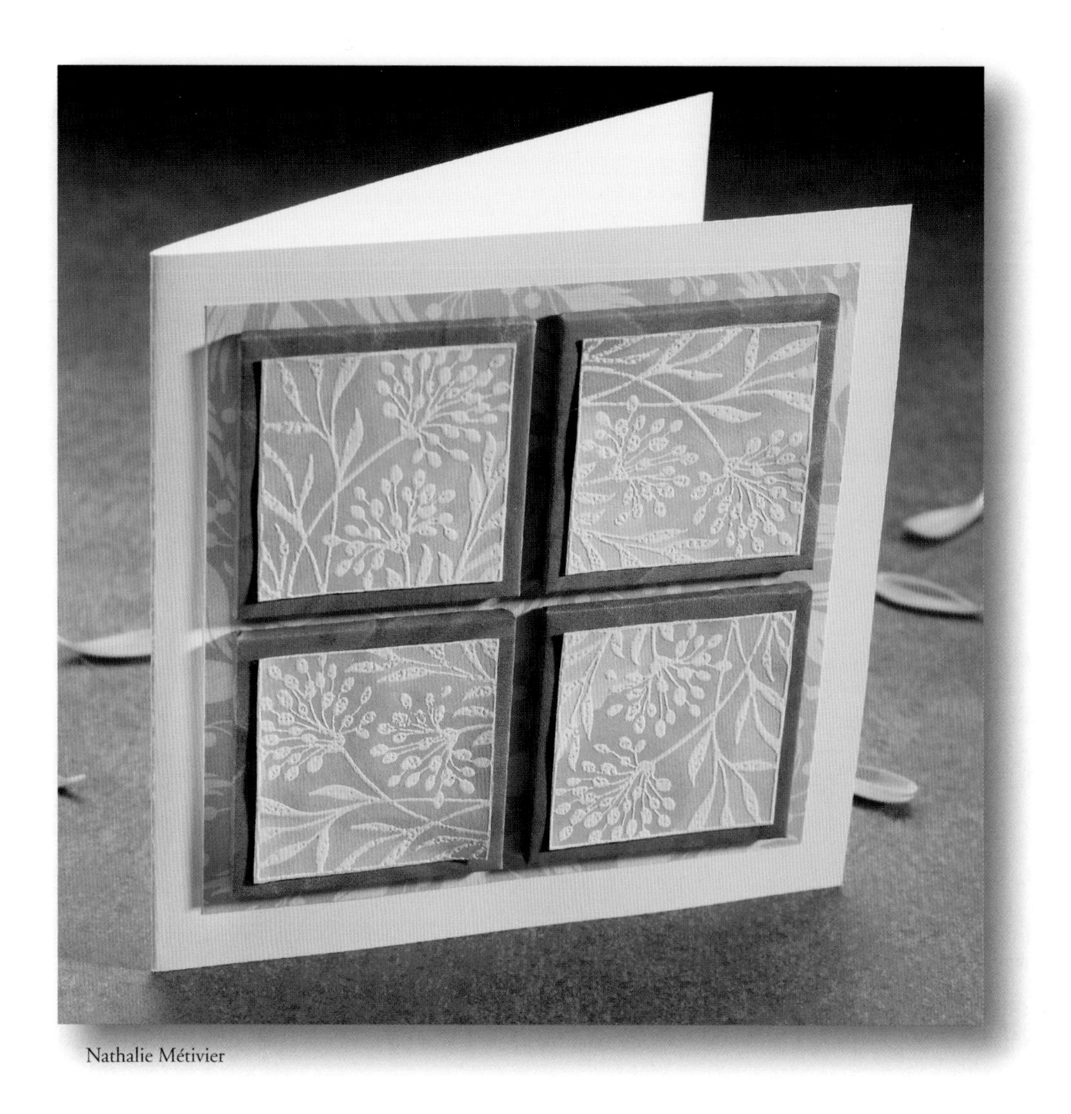

Nathalie Métivier

EMBOSSING—WHITE-ON-WHITE

The deep-etched rubber beds of Magenta stamps produce exquisite lines—lines that take color beautifully, offering crisp, clean edges. The faux watercolor summery palette of green and pink is gently brushed onto white-embossed cardstock swirling each color into the next. The image, stamped with white ink on white cardstock and embossed with white embossing powder, resists the added color and, when set with a heat tool, rises above the color wash with an intriguing texture of white lines amid a wash of color. Watercolor can produce many intriguing effects depending on what it is layered on and what is layered on it.

CREATING THE PROJECT

1. Stamp the image four times with white pigment ink on white cardstock. Cover the images with white embossing powder, being sure to tap any excess powder back into the container. Set the embossing with a heat tool. Brush water-based markers (Marvy) on a palette. Apply the ink by wetting the brush with lots of water, gathering some of the color from the palette, and brushing the color on the stamped, embossed cardstock. Apply the color quickly because it dries fast. It might be best, if you are new to this technique, to complete one tile at a time, rather than trying to paint one color on each tile before moving to the next color.

2. While the faux watercolor is drying, prepare the four cardboard tiles. Cut the turquoise printed paper to four 3-inch squares, trimming the corners in a slight reverse arc to create flat folded (non-bulky) corners when covering the cardboard tiles with the cut paper. Glue opposite sides first for a smooth fit of paper over the tile.

3. Cut each embossed square just outside the border. You want to keep the white raised border around each tile when it is mounted on the cardboard tiles just prepared in step 2.

4. Mount the trimmed embossed squares onto the wrapped cardboard tiles. Layer a 4 ½-inch square of Green Berry Branch printed paper on a 5 ¼-inch square card. Attach the four mounted cardboard tiles to the card.

Nathalie Métivier

EMBOSSING—WHITE-ON-BLACK

An outline image stamped with white pigment ink on black cardstock, embossed with white embossing powder and set with a heat tool, produces a stunning raised white outline against a black background. The iridescent watercolor inside the white embossed lines of the image together with the soft ribbons add a shimmering luxury to the gift tag. The raised—embossed—white outline resists the watercolor painted on top of it. This project is quick and easy, making it possible to create several tags in one session.

CREATING THE PROJECT

1. Cut black cardstock and white cardstock to 2 ½ by 4 ¾-inch panels. Cut printed paper to a 2 ½ by 3-inch panel. Stamp the Floral Tag image in ColorBox Frost White ink on the black cardstock panel. Emboss with white embossing powder, tapping any excess powder back into its container for future use. Emboss with a heat tool.

2. Paint the flowers with the iridescent inks in the watercolor palette as shown. Use just a small amount of water to apply color evenly and to keep the colors opaque. More water would make the painted image more translucent than we wished. Experiment to see what you prefer.

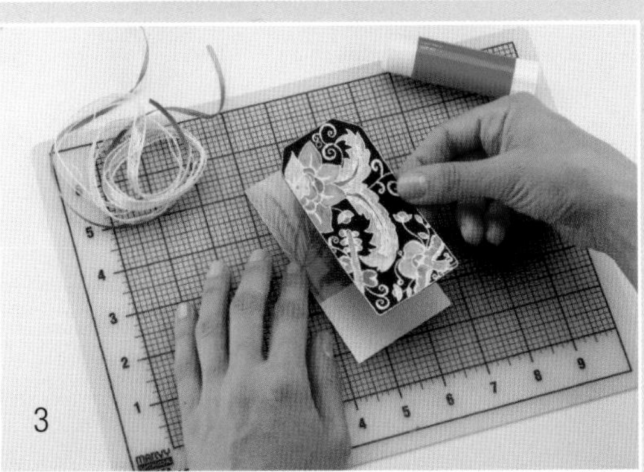

3. Cut around the tag shape with scissors. Mount the printed paper on the white cardstock panel, aligning the printed paper at the top of the white cardstock. Adhere the stamped, embossed, painted black tag to the printed paper panel, leaving a narrow border all around.

4. Cut the top corners of the bottom layer at an angle, and round the bottom corners. Punch a small hole at the top of the tag. Add the green ribbon, and finish with several loops of the iridescent ribbon. If you wish, add lightweight string to attach the tag to a package.

FOLDING

Paper can be beautifully manipulated. It is a rich, sensuous material that reponds to the touch. Explore the exciting assortment of folding techniques—origami, accordion folding, tea-bag folding, iris folding, squash folding, pockets, and pleating. There is something wondrously appealing about the added dimension of a folded project. The texture and weight in the folded segments, the play of light and shadow, the increased depth of the page appeal to one's imagination.

From simple to complex, a folded object offers great fascination. In this chapter we offer a variety of folded-paper craft projects—imaginative cards, tags, boxes, box toppers, bags, and even a wreath of folded/squashed tissue-

paper flowers to hang on your wall. Or use the tissue-paper flowers as decorative embellishments for a special gift. Whether the folds are few or many, streamlined or complicated, they add dimension and drama to your projects. Embellishments, those decorative accents that add extra style, are especially delightful when created with folded paper.

If you have a favorite design, there is no reason you can't turn to it over and over again. Use your imagination to change the components and the palette to change the look of the card. With a little creativity you can alter the composition and see a whole range of possibilities. Stretch your imagination and have fun.

Leslie Carola and Judy Ritchie

Origami Boxes

Three origami boxes were folded using the template on page 86, with three different sized squares of decorative paper—7 by 7 inches, 8 by 8 inches, and 10 by 10 inches. You can fold the boxes from almost any size square of paper. Fold the box top with a square of paper ¼ inch larger than the bottom (7 ¼ x 7 ¼ inches for the first box, for example). Paper is an extraordinary tool: It responds to the folds depending on its weight and texture. The flowers on top of these boxes were folded or squashed from different kinds of paper: a slightly stiff vellum with tiny printed squares scattered occasionally across the sheet, green printed cardstock, and white text-weight paper.

Paper Flowers

Variations on a theme: The pleated disc on the giftwrap (right) is started by accordion folding a strip of decorative paper—the same paper cut into narrow strips and used as a ribbon to wrap the package. The flower is completed by tying a thin wire around the middle of the accordion-folded strip of printed paper, pulling the ends together and gluing or attaching them with double-sided tape. This accordion-folded disc has a slightly deeper fold than the medallion.

Leslie Carola

CREATING THE PROJECTS (OPPOSITE)

For the green patterned medallion:

1. Score every ¼ inch along the long side of a 1 ¼ by 12-inch piece of decorative paper.

Accordion fold on the scores.

2. Trim one end of the folded strip to glue one panel over the other.

3. Pinch the folds together, gathering into a flat disc. Glue a small piece of cardstock to the back of the circle to hold the pleated circle medallion together. Trim the back piece as necessary.

4. Attach a decorative embellishment to the front center of the medallion.

Text-weight paper squashed flowers:

1. Punch nine same-size circles with scalloped edges. Place the circles, one on top of the other, on a soft surface (a piercing pad or a mouse pad) to create a stack of circles.

2. Pierce a hole in the center of the stack with an awl; insert a brad and fasten it in the back. Gather each layer of the punched circles one at a time, starting with the top layer, pulling and squashing it up around the centered brad. Bring each successive layer up to squash with the preceding layers around the brad, applying pressure to pull the layers together.

3. When all nine layers are squashed up around the brad, gently pull and push the layers to shape the layered bloom. A pointed tweezers may help to separate sections.

Anastasia Bosakowski

Folded Flowers

This handsome wreath is composed of thirty-five tissue paper roses in autumnal colors gathered and attached to a wreath frame with floral wire and a glue gun. The crafter deserves innumerable accolades for persevering with this large project. For the roses you will need tissue paper, floral wire, and a pair of scissors. For the wreath, a 12-inch wreath form, a spool of wired ribbon, thirty-five paper flowers, a hot glue gun, and three sticks of hot glue. Be very careful with the hot glue gun. Note: Do not let children play with a hot glue gun.

To make the flowers, gather a stack of six 4- by 6-inch sheets of tissue paper. Accordion fold the stack to eight folds, and round the ends with scissors. Cut a piece of floral wire 20 inches long, fold it in half, and wrap it around the center of the accordion-folded stack to hold the stack in place, leaving several inches of the wire hanging. Fan out the paper; pull one ply at a time toward the center, alternating sides as you work through the layers of paper. Trim the extra wire when the flower is completed. Attach to a package by tying the wire around the ribbon or attach the flower with foam dots or your choice of adhesive.

Anastasia Bosakowski

CREATING THE PROJECT

1. Wrap a 12-inch wreath form in ribbon using a dot of hot glue every other loop to hold the ribbon in place.

2. Take a 12-inch piece of ribbon and make a hanging loop with it. To do this, tie it into a closed circle with the wreath form linked into it. Make sure the knot is as far down the ribbon as possible. Seal it with glue and trim the ends. Place the knot against the inside of the wreath form and loop the ribbon around to make another knot on the outside of the wreath form, pulling the knot as close to the wreath form as possible to make a strong hanging loop.

3. One at a time, place the flowers on the wreath form, wrapping the wire around the wreath form. Glue the wire down in a few places, holding the wire until the glue sets (the wire won't stay in place otherwise). Place the flowers close enough together to hide the wreath form, but not so close that they get smashed together. Work your way around until the wreath is entirely covered.

4. Wrap a ribbon around the bottom of the wreath, between the flowers, and tie a bow.

One, two, or three flowers can decorate any number of projects—cards, boxes, frames, and so on.

Judy Ritchie

Novelty Folding

An informal card with a decorative pinwheel in carefree summery colors delights with an appealing palette, paper, and structure. Though some might think the simple centered composition formal, the informality of the colors dominates. We respond to color emotionally; it is probably the first element to capture our attention. The strong diagonally folded elements of the eight motion-filled arms are full of energy and fun.

CREATING THE PROJECT

1. Cut a 3 by 3-inch square panel of double-sided decorative paper.

2. Mark the center of each side. Find the center of the square and draw a ½-inch circle around it.

3. Mark a spot ⅝ inch on either side of the center of each side of the square. Crop off each corner of the square between the marks closest to each corner. An octagon with 1 ¼-inch sides remains.

4. Cut from each point of the octagon to the edge of the circle at the center of the octagon. This creates 8 triangles attached at the edge of the ½-inch circle.

5. Fold over the right side of each triangle two-thirds across the top of the triangle. You will have 8 flag-like shapes with a bright solid color on one side and bright multi-colored verso.

6. Add an embellishment (we used a button) to the center and adhere the pinwheel to a card. Add a type panel if desired.

Judy Ritchie

Easy place cards for a summer outdoor supper. Punch a few stars of various sizes from several different colored sheets of cardstock. We chose red, ivory, and blue cardstock for a 4th of July celebration. Score from and between each point of a punched star into the center of the star. Create mountain folds by pinching from each point into the center of the star. Valley folds will automatically form between the arms. Pinch the mountain folds several times to set the folds. The alternate mountain and valley folds allow the star to rest on the table with some dimension. Add name tags by cutting decorative paper in the shape of an elongated banner, write a name, wrap and glue the banner around the top of a toothpick. Insert the toothpick into the base of the star and add a small button or bead beneath the star to steady it.

Irene Seifer

Tea-Bag Folding

Sophisticated black and gold papers are folded in a simple form and arranged into a handsome topper for a box, card, or even a hanging ornament if two are created and attached back-to-back with a string or cord slipped between the two elements. An antique button anchors our mounded arrangement at the center. We added support to the bottom layer of folded shapes with heavy cardstock cut into the diamond shape, necessary only if your folding paper is lightweight. See the Diamond Fold template on page 87.

CREATING THE PROJECT

1. Cut eight 1 ½-inch squares of gold paper.

2. Cut sixteen 1 ½-inch squares of black and gold flower paper. Cut eight of the finished diamond fold shapes from a heavyweight gold paper to support the folded petals.

3. Use the Diamond Fold template on page 87 to fold the shapes.

4. Arrange the shapes in a three-tiered flower petal motif, starting by gluing the first eight black and gold folded shapes to the gold cut shapes. Add the last eight folded black and gold shapes, rotating slightly to overlap the first tier, and finally add the gold shapes, gluing all at the center. Finish with a decorative button at the center.

Irene Seifer

Tea-bag folding consists of folding shapes from small squares of paper to assemble in a decorative, dimensional motif. This wheel-like arrangement of red and gold diamond-shaped petals is anchored with a gold good-luck charm at its center. An elegant controlled palette, strong geometric shapes (circles, squares, triangles/diamonds), and a classic symmetrical design contribute to a pleasing, harmonious presentation.

CREATING THE PROJECT

1. The palette for this project is strong and unifying. The three papers—one crinkled metallic gold, one red and gold, and one red, gold, and white—repeat the colors of the mats and the large circular window through which we see the artful arrangement of folded papers. Fold a total of fifteen Diamond Fold tea-bag shapes, five with each of the three papers, following the folding instructions on page 87.

2. Arrange the folded diamonds in an overlapping circle on a white textured cardstock panel. Mat the panel with crinkled metallic gold and mount on the white card. Add a red square frame with a circular window cut to barely clear the outer edge of the circle of folded diamonds. Anchor the center of the circle with a gold Asian Happiness coin.

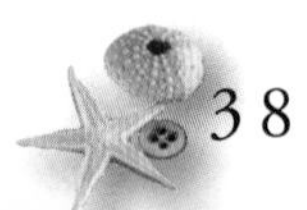

Susan Swan

Boldly printed papers add texture and interest to folded projects. You can incorporate many sizes and shapes of folded papers into unique and memorable designs. Use the folded components in a variety of ways—as a card, a tag, or a topper for a gift package. Text-weight paper is probably the easiest though not the only paper to work with. This inspiring artist designs her own papers and keeps them on her computer to use as she wishes. This project was created using the Petal Fold template on page 88.

Irene Seifer

The elegant tea-bag-folded ornament here was made using two different papers, one red and gold patterned and one black and gold patterned. A gold open-fan charm embellishes the center of the ornament. It is a variation of the Star Square Fold template on page 90. The palette and the interlocking shapes are dramatic, and the composition is elegant. This is a package that brings many gifts.

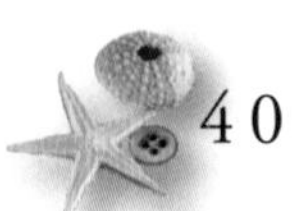

Irene Seifer

The tea-bag-folded ornament at the center of this project would be equally effective alone as the decoration on a card, or even in a smaller version on a tag. The ornament was made using the Star Square Fold template on page 90. The folded corners, made with the Double Kite Fold template on page 89, add an attractive finishing touch to the package. The palette and the interlocking shapes are clean and strong, and the composition is pleasing. A strong palette and simple shapes are the focus of most tea-bag-folded pattern.

ACCORDION FOLDING

Judy Ritchie

A stepped accordion-folded card with a charming beach pail, shovel, and sand castle punched along the top edge offers a special invitation to a birthday party. The staggered height of the panels and the shaped edge add interesting dimension. The ribbon stretching across all three panels anchors the design.

CREATING THE PROJECT

1. Cut cardstock to 12 (width) by 6 (height) inches. Score at 4-inch intervals along the 12-inch width to create three panels.

2. Cut the top diagonally from the upper left corner of the 12-inch side across to a 4-inch height on the 6-inch side.

3. Accordion fold and unfold vertically where scored to create three panels all the same 4-inch width but heights ranging from 6 inches at the left scaling down to 4 inches at the right.

4. Starting at the far right, punch the birthday candle edger twice at the top edge of each of the three 4-inch panels of the card. There will be a small section— about ¼ inch—of unpunched paper between the panels where you have punched the edger. Using a craft knife, trim away the unpunched paper left between the panels of the top edge.

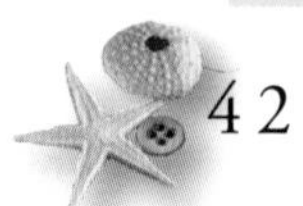

Here is a trifold card with differing width panels rather than the panels of differing heights as in the card opposite. Start this with a mountain fold so the fronts of the successively smaller panels are all visible from left to right. Scorefold the card into five sections, starting from the left: two at 2 ¼ inches wide, two at 3 ¼ inches wide, and one at 4 ¼ inches wide. Stickers and die-cut shapes decorate the edges of the staggered accordion-fold card.

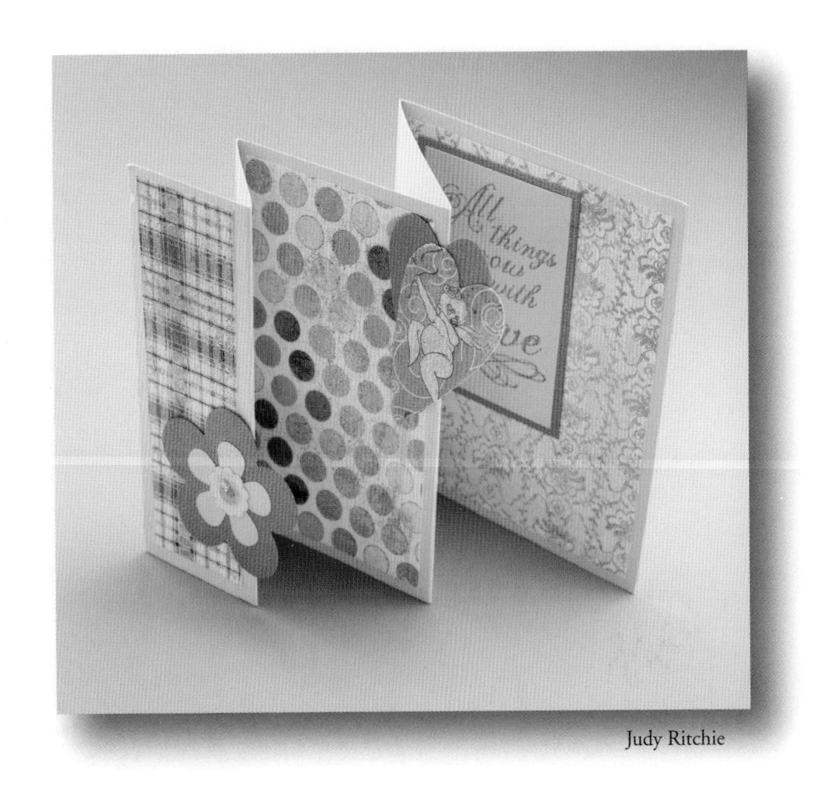

Judy Ritchie

Judy Ritchie

Start the accordion folding of this card with a valley fold, followed by a mountain fold. See the template on page 89 for this card made from a 12 by 12-inch sheet of two-sided cardstock. Four stamped and decorated tags slip into the pockets, and extra embellishments of ribbons, punched flowers, and a small type tag compete the job. The card is a lovely way to offer gifts like theater or concert tickets, dinner reservations etc.

Susan Swan

Iris-Folding

The cover of a vintage book of fairy tales inspired this card; the texture, shape, and soft color contribute to a vintage look. Even the style of the paper crafts signal a bygone time.

There are two folding projects here: a frame on the window cut into the front of the card extends from the back through the window to decorate the front, and an iris-folded frame inside surrounds a photo of a beautiful child.

CREATING THE PROJECT

Create an iris-folded mat using the template on page87, and layer it over the mounted photograph. Cut decorative paper to line the whole interior of the card, leaving a ¼-inch border all around the decorative paper liner. To create the two windows, draw appropriate-sized rectangles on the interior liner paper and on the card front. Be sure that the windows are aligned. Cut an X diagonally from inside corner to inside corner of the drawn window rectangle on the liner paper. Fold each triangle back over the straight edge of the window and pull it through the front window to create an interesting triangle frame. The multi layers add a distinctive touch.

Irene Seifer

Iris folding, like tea-bag folding, is a crafting technique from the Netherlands. The name reflects its similar look to the iris of an eye or a camera lens—narrow layers of folded paper arranged in an overlapping spiral pattern with a central opening. The layering creates appealing designs. The iris frame for this card closes in to a narrower central opening than the iris frame on the card opposite. This iris-folded tag is glued onto the ribbon that wraps around the card, tying at the right side. The palette is crisp, the design classic, and the composition pleasing. Use Iris Folding template on page 87. The card is a simple gatefold held closed by the ribbon and iris-folded tag.

Cutting

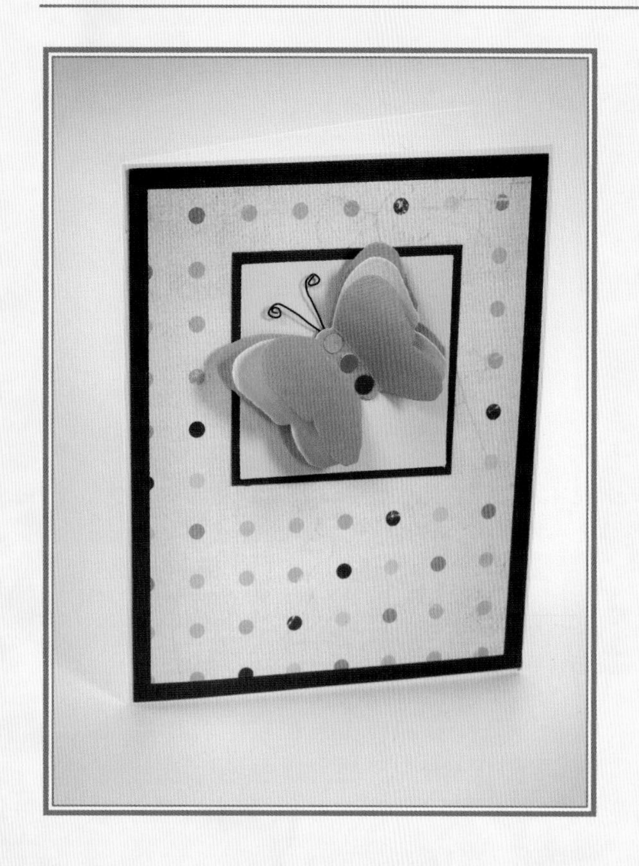

A few snips with scissors from decorative papers offer endless surprises. And don't forget the simple mat knife and ruler, tools that should be in every crafter's arsenal. Assembled letterforms or free-form shapes cut from colorful papers are delightful embellishments for cards, tags, or packages. One cut or punched shape alone on a card can be stunning. Layer one shape on top of another and it is very appealing. Layer again onto another shape and you have something remarkable. Windows cut into a card add dimension and texture. And punches, those marvelous handheld paper cutters, produce perfect shapes every time. Die-cutting machines—either electronic, like Cricut, or manual, like Cuttlebug or Sizzix—have become very popular with paper

crafters. Layering punched or die-cut shapes, whether in a classic symmetrical pattern or a carefree montage, is almost addictive!

Cut paper into small pieces, assemble them to construct a new form; make a few simple snips to release a surprise in the original shape; cut the paper into a new shape altogether; or tear paper carefully to release a sumptuous soft edge for an appealing decorative accent. Crisp, clean-edged punched or die-cut shapes on a card, tag, box or bag, or even on their own, provide an attractive design element. The positive and negative shapes (the shape left in the paper from which the shape has been cut) are useful. Layering is as useful to artful paper crafters as it is to fashionistas.

Judy Ritchie

Cutting and Layering

Three butterflies punched from three different, harmonious-colored cardstocks are layered for the look of a flier in motion. Sitting on a window of a light cardstock square layered onto a slightly larger brown mat, mounted on a large patterned and narrow brown mat before attaching to a soft ivory card. Color and texture are everything. The first butterfly, bright orange, is attached to the cardstock square by gluing only the body to the square, with the wings left free and lifted up. Each of the next two butterflies (one yellow and one light orange) is added the same way, attaching the body only and lifting each wing separately. Add three tiny punched circles down the length of the body for a colorful accent. We made the antennae from floral wire.

Judy Ritchie

A black patterned background is wondrously dramatic. The palette is sophisticated—black, burnt umber, and deep sandy tan; the texture almost palpable with the undulating curves of the cut rose, the crisp edges of the popped, matted art, and the textural look of the background paper. To create this embellishment, stamp the outline rose from Memory Box four times on lightweight white cardstock. Silhouette each rose at a different size by cutting on the line of a layer of petals. Squash each layer separately. Spray the four silhouetted roses with SmoochSpritz, a pearlized accent spray from ClearSnap. The spray softens the paper to aid the shaping of the rose. When dry, the paper stiffens with a glistening finish. Layer the petals with the largest section at the bottom getting successively smaller to the top. Insert a brad at the center. Tie a narrow ribbon across the bottom third of the black print panel and tuck the ends between the black patterned mat and the card. Attach the rose. Pop the layered wall art.

Irene Seifer

Punched or cut leaves gathered into a structured center arrangement provide a strong focal point on the front of this simple folded portfolio/card. The mound of red leaves accented with a few veined green leaves is centered on a silver cardstock mat and then layered onto a slightly larger red cardstock mat. The layered arrangement is adhered to the front of a dark green folded portfolio, on top of a decorative ribbon glued across the front and back of the folded card. We folded the portfolio from a 12 by 12-inch sheet of cardstock using the folding template on page 89. This is an attractive presentation for a simple gift—craft supplies, theatre tickets, a gift card, or a few memorable photographs.

CREATING THE PROJECT

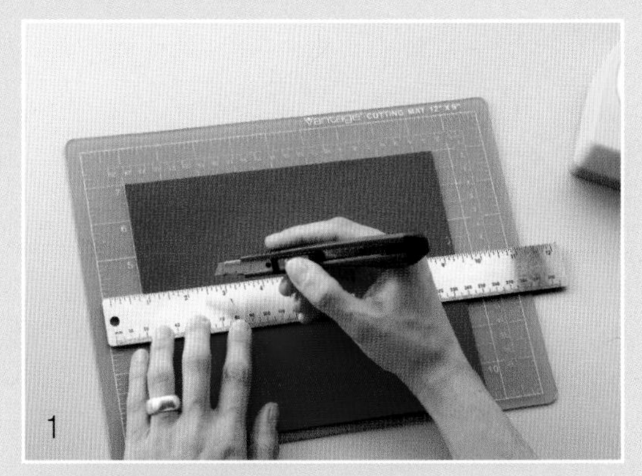

1. Cut a 5-inch square red cardstock panel. Cut a 4 1⁄2-inch square silver cardstock panel.

2. Punch ten leaves from red cardstock, and four leaves from dark green cardstock using a large leaf punch. We used a five-leaf punch from Punch Bunch. Punch a small sun shape to mix with glitter for the flower center.

3. Lightly score veins on the red and green leaves with an awl.

4. Assemble the pointsettia leaves on the silver cardstock mat; embellish the center with a small punched sun plus tiny jewels and glitter; attach to the red mat. Fold the portfolio from a 12-inch square sheet of green cardstock. Flatten the portfolio and place (see the completed portfolio interior, opposite) face down on your work surface. Glue a ribbon horizontally across the portfolio front and back, leaving long strands at each end to tie a bow. Adhere the matted constructed pointsettia on top of the ribbon. Tie a bow to close the portfolio.

Susan Swan

Corrugated pillow boxes embellished with lavish layers of punched flowers and a butterfly punched from colorful papers spark our senses. The varying sizes, the mixture of colors, the different textures, and the carefree tangle of shapes contribute to the flurry of motion and a feeling of well-being. The message is clear: don't be afraid to mix and match colors, shapes, and sizes for an exciting effect.

Judy Ritchie

The carefree arrangement of the blooms on the pearlized cardstock pillow box shouts of summertime fun. Every flower is at least two-toned: petals one color and the flower center another: light pink on deep rose, brown on yellow, peach on pink, and green-and-white polka dot leaves. Each yellow daisy is actually two punched flowers layered one over the other, attached at their centers. The petals are cut down toward the center of the flower. The ends of the petals are colored with chalk to add texture and shadows.

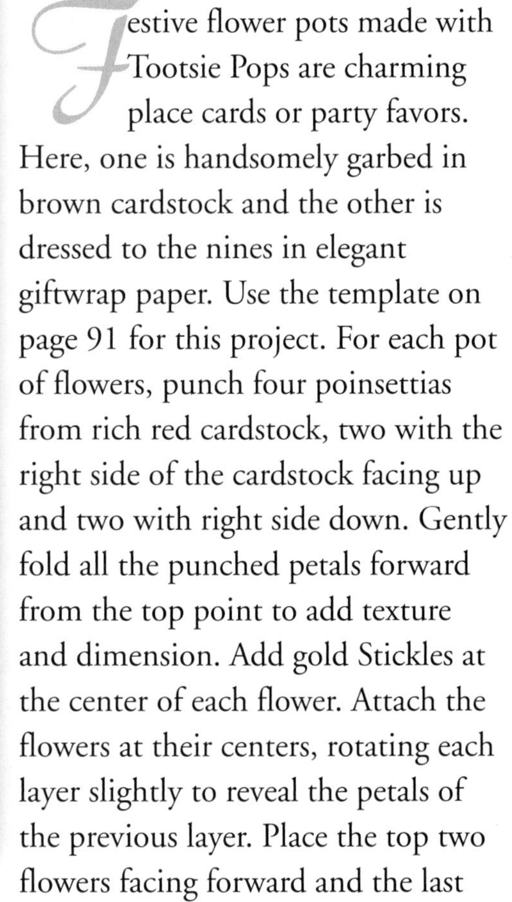

Judy Ritchie

Back-to-Back

Festive flower pots made with Tootsie Pops are charming place cards or party favors. Here, one is handsomely garbed in brown cardstock and the other is dressed to the nines in elegant giftwrap paper. Use the template on page 91 for this project. For each pot of flowers, punch four poinsettias from rich red cardstock, two with the right side of the cardstock facing up and two with right side down. Gently fold all the punched petals forward from the top point to add texture and dimension. Add gold Stickles at the center of each flower. Attach the flowers at their centers, rotating each layer slightly to reveal the petals of the previous layer. Place the top two flowers facing forward and the last two facing away so that the arrangement is "finished" when viewed from all sides. The upside-down Tootsie Pop stick, wrapped in green paper, provides the stem, while its edible head tucked inside the pot stabilizes the structure. A holiday bow decorates the front of each pot.

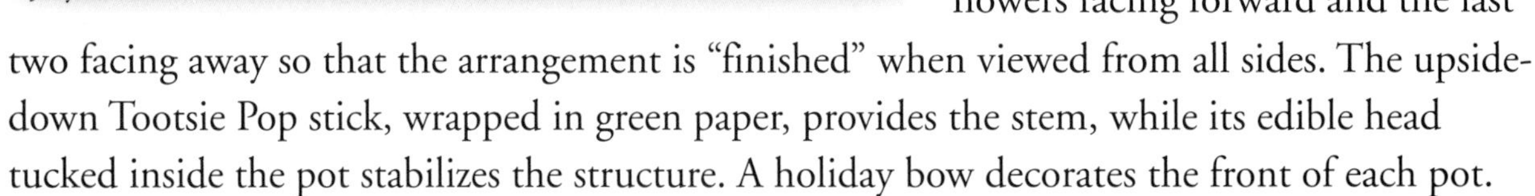

For a summertime version, punch two flowers from a bright solid cardstock and one patterned for each flower pot. Fold the punched solid flower petals from the indent at the top of each petal diagonally down to the outside edge of the petal. Fasten the blooms back-to-back with the patterned bloom between. Embellish the flower centers as you wish.

Leslie Carola

One large glittering white snowflake fills a window in a midnight-blue card. A window card can be so simple and elegant. This snowflake—two punched snowflakes fastened back-to-back on a taut monofilament—stretches the height of the window. Cut two card fronts with windows. One will serve as the liner (to cover the wire) after you attach the hanging snowflake. The snowflake dances as you open the card. The window cut in this card is decorative and functional, adding an extra dimension.

Karen Lockhart

Cutting the Card

Concentrating on cutting only the main image of a card or tag limits the possibilities. Here are two cards with cut decorative edges, adding great style to the projects. Details tell a story. The simple detail of the cherry leaf extending beyond the frame is an elegant touch. A few snips with scissors and you add texture, dimension, and style. The ice-cream cone is stamped, colored, silhouetted, and popped on a punched mat. Raising a silhouetted image from the surface is another refined, simple technique. The card and tag each has a punched edge backed by patterned paper. The message here is that altering a card or tag shape itself is an engaging detail, adding texture and dimension.

Susan Swan

Color and texture are prominent details—whether a calm, elegant white-on-white offering or a cheerful display of butterflies and flowers in an energizing palette. The monochromatic card uses texture as an appealing, almost-sculptural device. A butterfly shape is punched out of the top right corner of the card front, as though the delicate flier has just left. Two more butterflies punched from lightly patterned white cardstock are attached to the card below the missing one, perhaps poised to depart as well. A handmade envelope with a ribbed lining continues the accent on texture, but with a hint of color.

A colorful collection of layered flower petal shapes is seen through a round window punched in the upper left corner of an ivory landscape-folded card. Silhouetted butterflies hover on the card front near the window to a mini garden. For delightful detail, each butterfly is punched twice, from different papers. The wings are trimmed away on the second shape. The remaining, silhouetted body is layered on the whole punched butterfly for an intriguing effect.

Judy Ritchie

Die-cut Images

Handheld punches create crisp, accurate cuts. When creating a negative shape—the shape left when you remove the positive shape—crafters are usually limited as to where on a card or sheet of paper they can punch the shape. The shape to be punched must be near an edge in order for the punch to reach the spot. Die-cutting machines allow crafters to cut a shape from a sheet, card, or tag wherever they choose. Personal die-cutting machines can be electronic, like Cricut, or manual, like Cuttlebug or Sizzix. Manual die-cutters still give you that hands-on creative process, while the electronic die-cutting machines rely on a click of a button. Each machine has its own way to operate, but the end result is crisp, clean shapes.

Judy Ritchie

A bare winter tree is die cut from brown cardstock and placed on a sky-blue mat. But this crafter chose to die cut the tree twice—once from a piece of brown cardstock and once from a light-blue cardstock mat cut to a size appropriate for the card size. The blue mat is left with the negative tree shape (the positive shape has been removed). The positive brown tree shape is fitted carefully inside the negative blue shape, creating a hint of texture—an elegant, simple step. For an interesting presentation, embellish the tree with Flower Soft tiny colored sprinkles. Put small dabs of glue on the areas of the tree where you want to add some colorful blooms. Sprinkle the Flower Soft over the glue and gently tap the excess back into the container. Let the card dry for twenty to thirty minutes.

Robert Carola

Cutting with Templates

Tags, bags, cards, and packages are all wonderful vehicles for delightful cut-paper animals. Use the template on page 93 to create this colorful owl constructed with Post-It [R] craft paper from 3M. The adhesive-backed paper layers smoothly. Here we have the steps to cut and layer the owl. Remember that you can enlarge or reduce the template as necessary to suit your project.

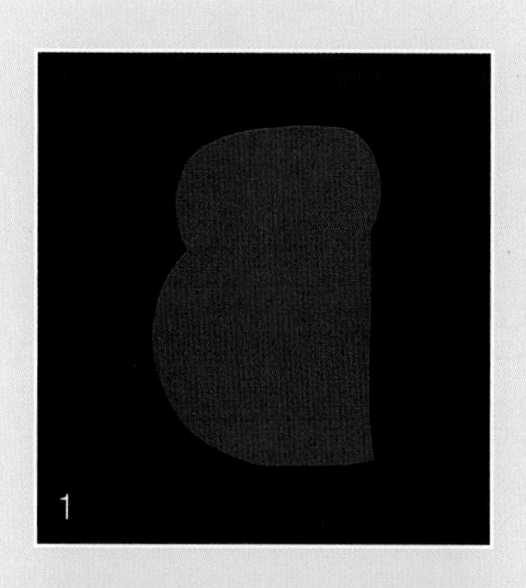

Creating the Project

1. Cut the body of the owl from dark blue paper.
2. We usually work with one or two colors per step. Add the hot pink wings, ears, and top of the head. The rest of the steps are created with circle punches plus a small cut triangle. Add the yellow buttons on the chest.
3. Add the large white eyes.
4. Add the purple eyelids, one punched circle cut in half.
5. Finish with a green triangle nose and black eyeballs, two punched black circles cut in half. See the finished owl above.

Robert Carola

You can have endless fun with small gift packaging. These delightful animals are guaranteed to bring a smile. See page 93 for templates for each of the animals, perfect for gift bags, cards, tags, invitations, place cards—whatever you can imagine. Enlarge or reduce the templates as appropriate.

We all respond instantly to color. The bright, cheerful cut-paper figure of the juggling octopus is layered directly on the bag. The individual pieces—head, eight arms, hat, and balls—are cut from Post-It^{R} craft paper from 3M.

The little mouse is cut from cardstock—silver metallic for the body, and purple, pink, and black cardstock for the tail, ears, and eyes. The mouse may be in traditional cool tones, but the charm of this wide-eyed little critter overrides our color response and makes us just as happy.

Susan Swan

FREE-HAND CUTTING

Various painted papers are used to create playful letters and a flower on a birthday card and envelope. The letters and flowers are layered onto glossy black paper. The front of the card is cut narrower than the back to reveal the flower at the right edge of the interior page. Cut a selection of brilliant papers (hand painted or commercial) into manageable sizes. Assemble various snippets of the cut paper shapes to create letters—all capital letters—to spell the message "Happy Birthday." Susan scanned her hand-painted papers, printed and cut them. She has the papers stored on her computer.

Susan Swan

A celebratory palette, a symmetrical design, and imaginative components offer an intriguing project. The giant birthday candles are imaginative while creating a strong composition. Everything angles to the center—a visually appealing, strong arrangement. The semi-circle window cut in the top front of this whimsically cheerful card allows us to see an arc of yellow stars against a black background on the interior page. When the card is opened those stars are revealed to be lit candles, the flames being the stars and the candles themselves tall, angled strips of painted pink paper stretching to the stars. The original paper was hand-painted and scanned in to the computer. The cutting was done in Photoshop on the computer, as was the type and the irregular edge at the top and sides. One could create this project by hand—painted papers scanned or not for cutting. But digital work is exciting and economical.

Special Effects

Special effects are all about embellishments, textural dimension—added bits and pieces that delight the eye. Sometime the paper itself is manipulated, other times new materials are added, or the papercraft can be affixed to another object. Whatever the process, the finished project has evolved from a simple slip of paper to an engaging artwork. The process is enjoyable for the crafter and certainly for the recipient.

In creating this chapter we have selected some projects that have captured our imagination. The categories are by no means complete, the offerings are merely samples of some pleasing papercrafting. We hope we have gathered a collection of projects that are pleasing to all. Quilling is the art of rolling

narrow strips of paper into coiled shapes and combining the shapes to form decorative designs. Some projects from Magenta appealed with their detail and dimensionality, from extraordinary coloring, their own special Peel Off's stickers and the addition of extra materials. Flowers of various sizes punched from hand-watercolored papers, Zentangled, and gathered into a tissue-wrapped bouquet affixed to a card is full of life. Two little mantle ladies, one celebrating Hannukah and one celebrating Christmas, are imaginative and charming. Collage using a fresh flower, fern, and twigs to frame demands attention. We show an alternate version side-by-side with a brilliant red tag instead of the woodland look. You choose. Embroidered ribbon flowers lend an old world grace to a project—not a bad idea.

QUILLING

Quilling—also known as paper filligree—is the art of rolling narrow strips of paper into coiled shapes and combining the shapes to form decorative designs. Filligree was popular among eighteenth century England's fashionable women who used the technique to decorate tea caddies, baskets, and even furniture. Colonists coined the term "quilling" and decorated boxes, trays, and other everyday items. Here it adorns a special package.

CREATING THE PROJECT

1. Cut a styrofoam globe in half and set aside.
2. Create dozens of tiny quilled pink, deep rose, and yellow roses using the instructions on page 92.
3. Punch leaves from light- and medium-green cardstock; add hand-drawn veins on the leaves in a medium green with a good quality marker.
4. Glue the punched leaves onto one of the styrofoam domes (half of a globe shape). Glue the quilled roses in clusters of three—one of each color—over the surface of punched leaves.
5. Mount the embellished dome on a pleated pink ribbon mat atop a wrapped gift box.

Janet Williams

SOME BASIC QUILLED SHAPES

LOOSE GLUED COIL

Roll the paper on the quilling tool to form a coil. Remove the coil from the tool. Allow the coil to relax and expand to desired size, and apply small amount of glue to the end of paper strip, gluing down to the coil.

TIGHT COIL

Roll the paper on the quilling tool to form a coil. DO NOT allow the coil to relax and expand. While the coil is still on the tool, apply small amount of glue to the end of paper strip, gluing down to the coil. Gently remove the coil from tool.

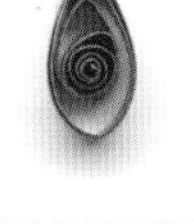

TEAR DROP

Make a loose glued coil. Pinch at one end of the coil to form a teardrop shape.

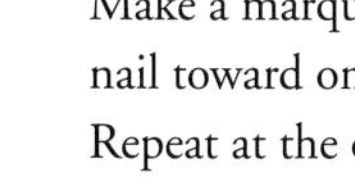

SHAPED MARQUISE

Make a marquise. Run your fingernail toward one point curling it up. Repeat at the other end curling in the opposite direction.

MARQUISE

Make a loose glued coil. Pinch at the exact opposite side of coil to form points at both ends, forming a marquise shape.

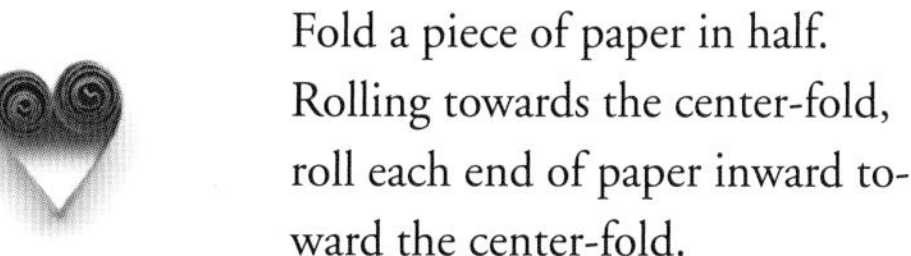

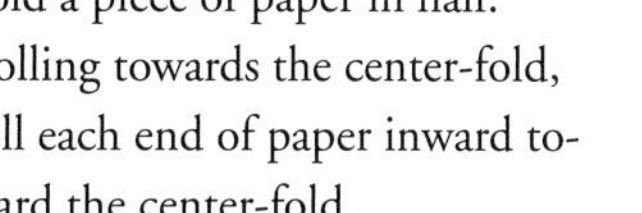

OPEN HEART

Fold a piece of paper in half. Rolling towards the center-fold, roll each end of paper inward toward the center-fold.

SHAPED TEARDROP

Make a teardrop. Run your fingernail toward the point curling the point in one direction.

SQUARE

Make a loose glued coil. Flatten the coil between your fingers. Hold the flattened coil upright between thumb and index finger with the points at the top and bottom. Flatten again matching up the previous 2 folds created by the points. Reopen to form a square shape.

HALF CIRCLE

Make a loose glued coil. Flatten one side of the coil by pinching the circle at two points or flatten coil gently against your finger.

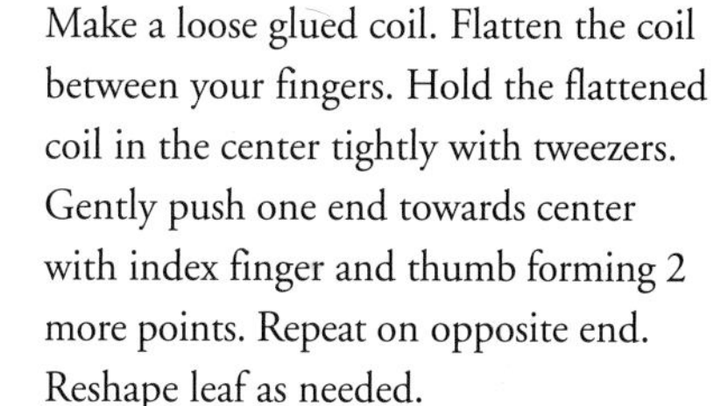

HOLLY LEAF

Make a loose glued coil. Flatten the coil between your fingers. Hold the flattened coil in the center tightly with tweezers. Gently push one end towards center with index finger and thumb forming 2 more points. Repeat on opposite end. Reshape leaf as needed.

ROLLED HEART (ARROW)

Make a teardrop. Hold the teardrop shape between the thumb and index finger of one hand. Gently push the center of rounded end back using the straight edge of the tweezers. Crease at both sides of the pushed-in end.

CRESCENT

Make a teardrop. Pinch one more point not quite opposite of the first point. Run your fingernail toward both points curling the points up or make a loose glued coil. Press coil against the rounded side of the quilling tool or finger to give the coil a crescent shape.

Janet WIlliams

This lovely holiday table decoration is created with quilled and die-cut shapes. A styrofoam tree shape is covered with dozens of die-cut leaves finished with hand-drawn veins, quilled green holly leaves, and quilled red berries scattered about. The gold star tree ornament, below, is a wood star covered with dozens of loose glued coils.

CREATING THE PROJECT

1. Die cut enough green leaves—two sizes— to cover the entire foam cone. Highlight veins with a green gel pen. Gently roll the leaf edges to add some texture. Beginning at the top of the cone, glue the leaves in place overlapping them slightly as they cascade down the cone.

2. Use 6- to 8-inch pieces of 1/16-inch wide green quilling paper to make ½ inch to ⅝-inch loose glued coils. To make a holly leaf, flatten a coil and grasp in the middle with tweezers. Pinch one pointed end and push backward toward the middle. Repeat on the other pointed end. Plump out the sides of the shape into a holly leaf. Glue holly leaves on top of randomly placed cut leaves.

3. Make loose coils from 1-inch pieces of 1/16-inch wide red quilling paper. Glue the "berries" next to the quilled holly leaves and add red crystal gems to highlight.

4. Punch out one star, glitter both sides with gold glitter, and glue the star to the top of the tree.

The stunning gold star Christmas tree ornament, above right, is something you can make for your own tree or for any lucky friend if you can bare to part with it! A purchased wood star ornament is painted gold and covered with tiny gold quilled loose glued coils.

Janet Williams

Three variations of ornaments—tree or gift package decorations—with quilled snowflakes. When making any snowflake, the size of the finished snowflake shape will be determined by the length of quilling paper. Increase and decrease the length of the paper to make the snowflake fit your base shape.

For the black snowflake, the shapes were made using 1- to 3-inch pieces of ⅛-inch wide gold-edged black quilling paper. The snowflake is made with the following shapes, working from the center out to the outside row. Make the shapes and assemble as shown: 1) Teardrop, 2)Marquise, 3) Heart from off-center "S" shapes, 4) Crescent, 5) Loose glued coil, 6) Teardrop. Glue the finished snowflake down on the porcelain disc. Highlight the edge of the disc with a gold paint pen.

Clear Glass Star Snowflake shapes were made using 1-to 3-inch pieces of ⅛-inch wide white quilling paper. Make the following shapes starting from the center out to the outside row and assemble on a glass star: 1) Marquise, 2) Heart, 3) Crescent 4) Teardrop, 5) Smaller Teardrop, 6) Loose glued coil. Spray the glass star with gold glitter spray and let dry. Glue the finished snowflake on to the star.

Janet Williams

Delicate quilled flowers and greenery embellish brilliant colored pigment-inked quail eggs, looking every bit like Russian Easter eggs nestled in their basket. The blown eggs are first colored with pigment inks and then the quilled flowers and leaves are glued to the dry eggs. Sumptuous colors, intricate paper filigree, and stunning textures contribute to the splendid effect. Quilled paper coils can be affixed to any surface that will hold glue. A pointed tweezers is a help grabbing and holding tight folds.

Janet Williams

Inexpensive household items can be upgraded with imaginative handmade decorations. A refined display of tiny purple and white quilled roses edged in silver nestled on punched green leaves adorns a silver ribbon wrapped around and crossed at the front of two small glass tea-light holders. Instructions for the quilled roses are on page 92.The textured shapes add delicate notes of color and dimension to a wide array of projects using many materials.

Nathalie Métivier

Textural Embellishments

This embellished frame consisting of one smaller frame resting on a larger one—combines an appealing palette, texture, and a classic composition. The colors in both frames echo those in the photograph. And the texture complements what we see in the photo. To hide the ends of the copper wire used to attach the beads, insert it into the foam between the two frames. The few copper leafy Peel Off's scattered in the background provide a spot of brilliance.

Magenta is a fine company known for their attention to details, and their own Peel Off's stickers are no exception. Available in several finishes, they provide beautiful color, pattern, and texture to a project. You can add color to the Peel Off's with permanent ink markers or alcohol ink for additional decorative effects. Start with a clear or colored glass ball and add Peel Off's with or without additional color. These brilliantly decorated glass Christmas tree ornaments show the fun to be had with these sophisticated stickers.

Nathalie Métivier

Nathalie Métivier

The luminous metallic pearl quality of this card with the chipboard bird is accomplished with coats of pearlescent watercolor. For the background, brush color on a chipboard frame with Distress ink (it dries quickly), stamp a ginko branch, and swirl over it with a translucent pearlescent watercolor (mixed with plenty of water to achieve the translucent look). Add Peel Off's (these are silver) and dab them unevenly with less-diluted pearlescent watercolors for more pronounced definition. The chipboard bird sports Peel Off's negative shapes of his own.

Susan Sheppard

Punched flowers of various sizes and shapes, decorated with Zentangle decorative doodles drawn in a fine black pen, and gathered into a tissue-wrapped bouquet send a lovely message. Select a few flower punches of different sizes. Cut watercolor paper into squares to accommodate the size of the punches selected. Cover both sides of the watercolor paper with watercolor pencils and paint with water. When both sides are dry, and the color is pleasing to you, punch the flowers. Add the repetitive line drawings with a fine Micron black pen. Add a card-stock stem to each flower, and wrap three together in tissue paper; embellish with black dots in the flower centers and a gold sticker on the wrap. Affix the bouquet to a panel and mat appropriately.

Susan Sheppard

Two cheerful box dolls, one dressed for Chanukah and one dressed for Christmas, perch on a mantle with narrow accordion-folded, decorative-paper arms holding tiny wrapped gifts, ribbon legs dangling, and tiny bell feet swaying. Created by a crafter with a delightful sensibility, the bodies of these disarming figures are made with small jewelry gift boxes standing on end and lined with appropriate-colored paper: the legs are blue or red ribbon strands, feet are tiny bells—one set silver, the other gold. The heads are stamped near the top edge of a cardstock panel that attaches to the back of the upturned box/body. Festive, joyous, and celebratory.

Susan Swan

Here we see the power of color. The main attraction—a collage of a dried white daisy on green ferns— layered onto a handmade rustic-looking sandy paper heart mat looks almost reserved in the natural twig frame. The same project on a bright red mat clamors for our attention. For the twig-framed project, mount the collage on checkerboard paper. Layer the checkerboard paper on a Bristol board or other heavyweight stock, and trim to the appropriate shape. Create a frame with four small twigs bound together with twine. Add a twine hanger with a dangling ornament made with rolled handmade paper and beads. Glue a small rectangle of gold foil at the center of the heart-shaped paper, layer the ferns and a dried flower on top. Add a strip of a music score for the flower stem. For the red matted version, mount the small collage onto a red lightweight board. Add a red cord through a hole punched at the top of the tag.

The fun-filled earring card is both the card and the gift: the earrings dangling from Mom's ears are real. They are the gift! But then, we couldn't say that the card is not a gift. The crafter has used a potpourri of materials, not to mention an intriguing folding process. The lace, button eyes, and small fabric rose are also real. The rest of the card was created on a computer, printed, and constructed. From left to right at the bottom of this page, we see the steps to create the elements of the card: a strip of checkerboard paper, a strip of lace, a small silk rose, painted letters "M o m," a piece of a scanned flower painting, and the painted paper card with a special fold in the front. Next is the head with earrings in place, followed by the finished head with cut-paper hair and button eyes. The assembled card is right, here. You do have to smile. Crafting is about celebrating life and having fun—fun for the crafters and recipients both.

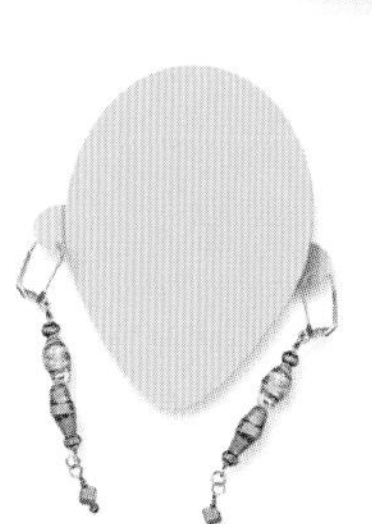

Susan Swan

Judy Ritchie

Simple Pop-Ups

Pop-ups are so appealing. And this one is so easy. A few cuts and folds using the template on page 87 create three stand up braces ready to support the disarming stamped, silhouetted owls. The card front is an appealing classic, centered layered composition in a warm, subtle palette. The interior offers three wise-looking, wide-eyed owls who pop out from a delicately stamped and over-stamped simple line, natural–looking environment as the card opens. The smallest owl, in the center, looks about to speak. The others are engaged in their own thoughts or feelings. The subtle palette projects a quiet tone.

Judy Ritchie

Susan Sheppard

Pop-up cards frequently look difficult to create but they are often surprisingly easy to do so. Plan and measure carefully before cutting and folding to make the task easier and more professional. Don't be afraid to experiment or vary the details. Accidents can be beneficial. Filled with fun and spunk, this disarming pop-up card uses simple folds.

Cut two cards, one from yellow and one from black cardstock. Cut black stripes for the yellow card. Lay the yellow card, front side up, on a work surface and glue the black stripes appropriately across the card. Fold and score the black card in horizontal quarters. While the black card is folded, punch a circular window through all four layers. Lay the black card with the cut port-

Susan Sheppard

hole-like windows over the yellow- and black- striped card and mark where the last window on the right is placed. Cut the window in the yellow-and black-striped layer (the front of the card) so you can see through to the back of the card. Turn the yellow striped card over and lay the black card with punched windows on top of it, face up. Lightly draw circles to indicate the placement of the windows on the verso side of the yellow-and-black stried card (the inside back of the yellow/black striped card). Stamp, color, and decorate figures in the three right-hand penciled circles. Erase the penciled circles. Glue the black card with four punched windows to the inside of panels one and four. Pull the top layer of the black card center into a mountain fold. Add a message on the card front if desired.

Irene Seifer

RIBBONERIE

Try something unexpected with your next project like embroidery on paper, using both silk ribbon and embroidery floss. These charming ribbon roses are eas to create and add soft texture to a project. Create a simple embroidery grid—a star shap with an uneven number of points—using embroidery floss. An uneven number of points guarantees alternate over and under placement on each point. Embroider the green leaves with embroidery floss using a lazy-daisy stitch.

CREATING THE PROJECT

1. Cut and fold lilac cardstock into a 5-inch square top-folded card. Cut a second piece of lilac cardstock to a 3-inch square. Cut white cardstock to a 4 ½-inch square panel, and a 2 ½-inch square panel.

2. Punch two holes in one corner of the 2 ½-inch square. Create the embroidery grid with an uneven number of points and a center dot. Mark the grid in pencil on the white cardstock panel Stitch from each point of the star in to the center with embroidery floss. Anchor the ribbon at the center of the grid and wind it over and under each thread spoke around the circle.

3. The stems and leaves are green embroidery floss. Slip a lilac ribbon in an out of the two punched holes at the top of the card-stock panel, and tie a bow.

4. Layer the panels.

Irene Seifer

Ribbon-embroidered yellow roses at the center of an embossed floral shape add a textural, elegant note. Create this ribbon embroidery just like the lilac card opposite. Once the ribbon embroidery flowers are finished, stitch the smaller yellow buds and green leaves with embroidery floss. See the photo of the steps on page 84.

Summery pink ribbon in puffy loops creates three dimensional flowers for a timeless card (foreground). Using an embroidery needle, bring the ribbon up from the back of the white cardstock panel from the outside edge of the flower and stitch down at the center. Do not pull tight. Pinch each of the five petals of the flowers to add dimension. Layered papers and a ribbon border are featured on the card at back.

Kim Smith

Irene Seifer

An elegant bridal shower is just the time to indulge in ribbon-embroidery decorative items. The linen napkins are embellished with pink ribbon-embroidered roses and greenery, as is the paper invitation and a keepsake accordion-fold teatime recipe booklet. The embroidery is easy. See above: trace the teapot onto white cardstock, create a template for the embroidery and sketch it on the teapot drawing. Place the drawn teapot with embroidery template on a sponge pad. Transfer the grid by poking holes in the teapot drawing with an awl, following the stitching template in place. Create the embroidery grid with pink (like the ribbon) embroidery floss. Stitch from each point of the star in to the center of the figure. Create the rose by pulling the ribbon over and under the stitched loops. Embroider the greenery.

Irene Seifer

This charming accordion-folded recipe booklet is a thoughtful memento for the guests and guest-of-honor. Accordion-fold enough sheets of cardstock to obtain the number of pages you want for your book. Print out the recipes, trim the pages, and glue the pages down to the leaves in your folded booklet. The cover offers the same ribbon-embroidered teapot shape used for all the components of this tea party.

Templates

ORIGAMI BOXES, page 30

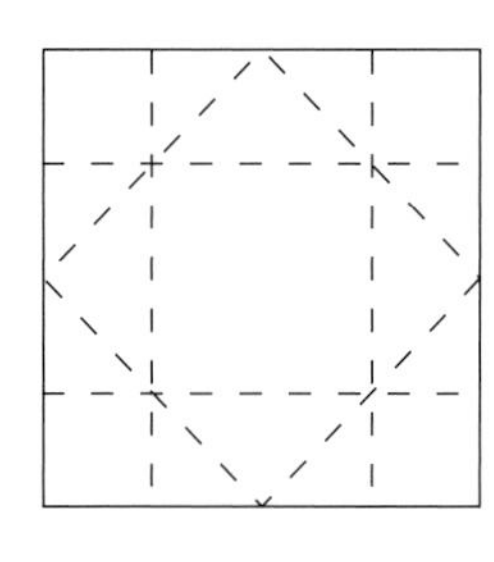

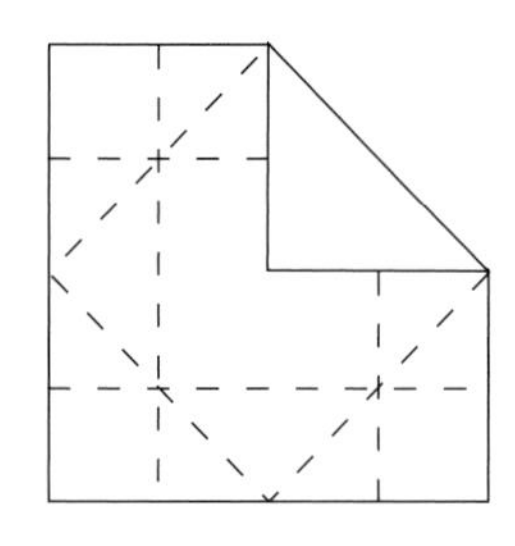

1. Start with a square paper. Fold all corners into center.

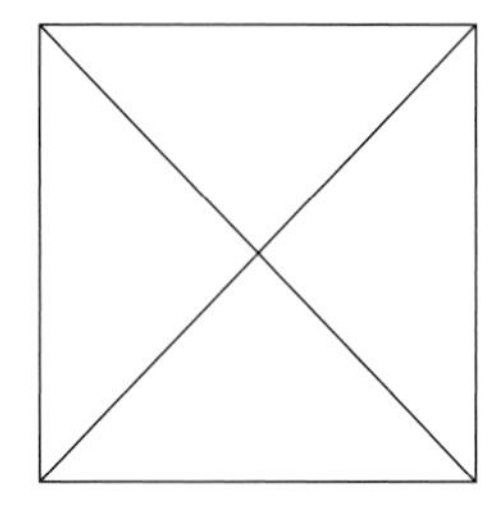

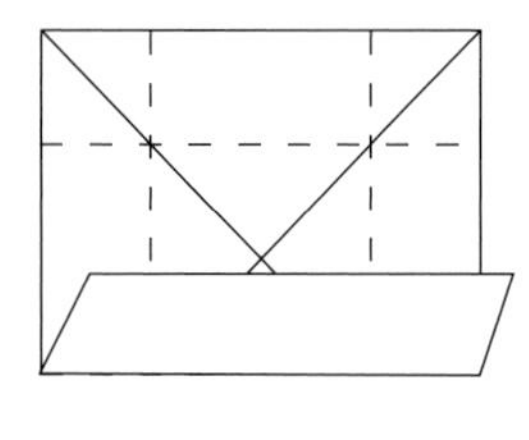

2. With all 4 corners folded to center, fold and unfold all straight edges to center to crease.

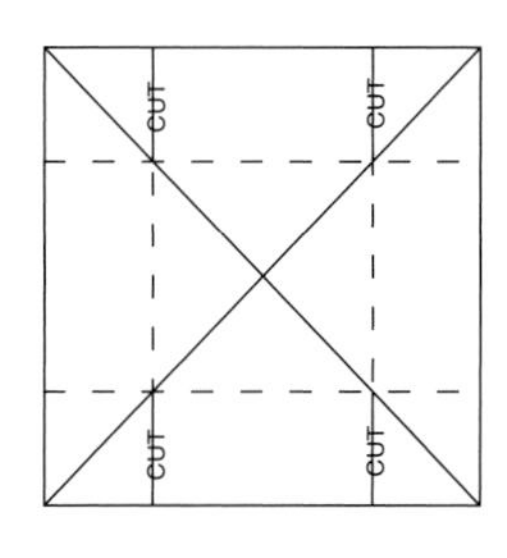

3. With corners still folded to center, cut only where indicated on diagram.

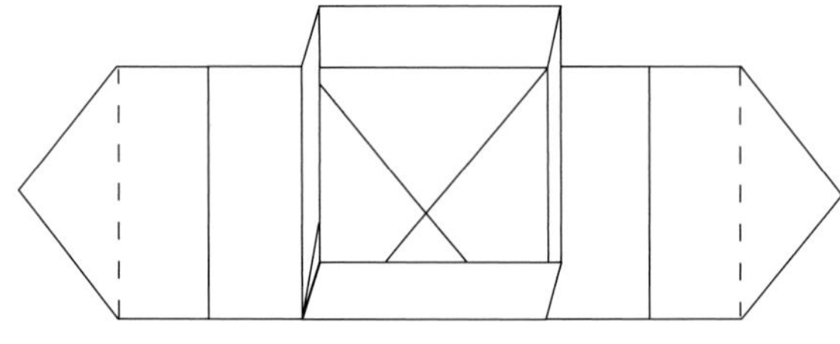

4. Unfold 2 opposite sides to form first 2 sides of box by standing up sides and overlapping excess.

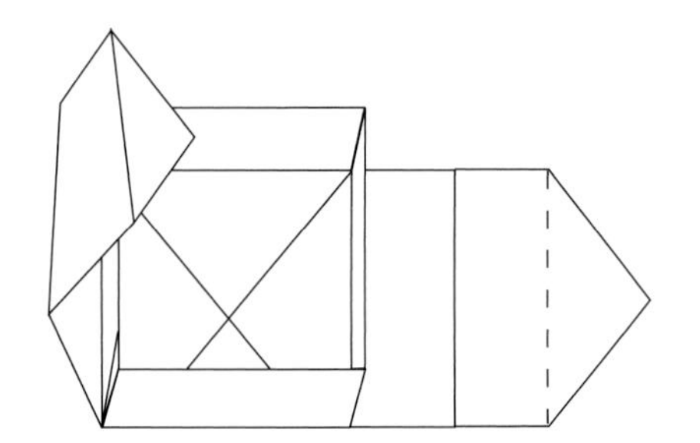

5. Fold remaining sides inward, over the existing sides and fasten to floor of box with a dab of glue stick.

Repeat steps 1-5 to make bottom of box using a 1/4" all around smaller paper.

DIAMOND FOLD, page 36

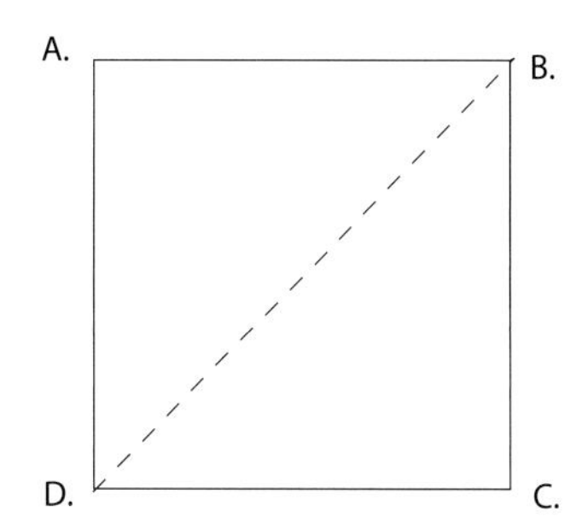

1. Fold the square in half diagonally. Crease and unfold.

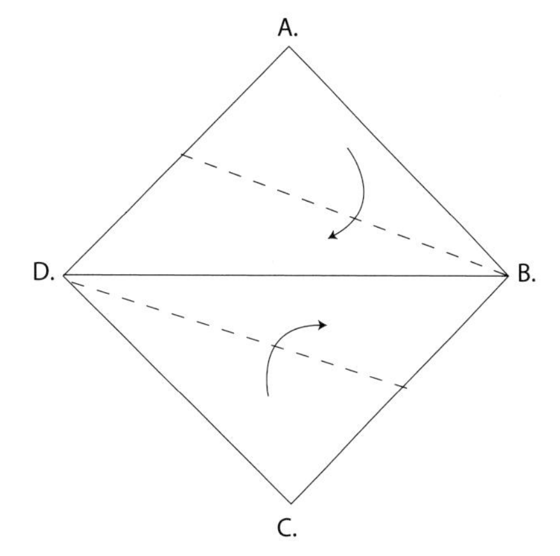

2. Rotate square 45° so point A is at top. Fold the A-B side in to center. Fold the C-D side to center.

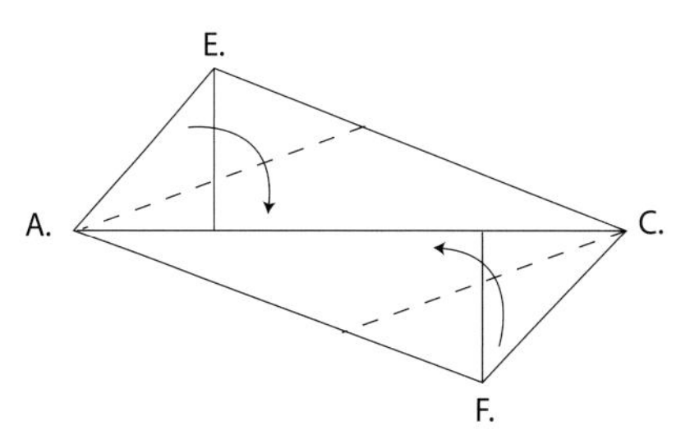

3. Fold the A-E side to center. Fold the C-F side to center.

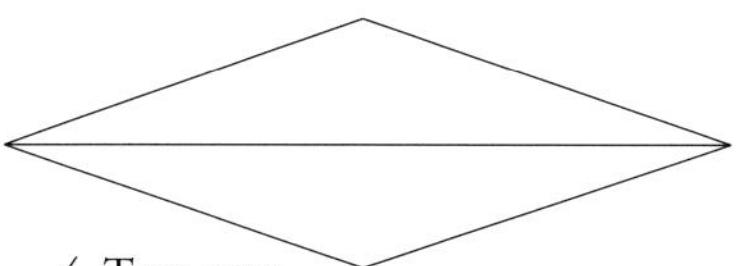

4. Turn over.

IRIS FOLD, page 42

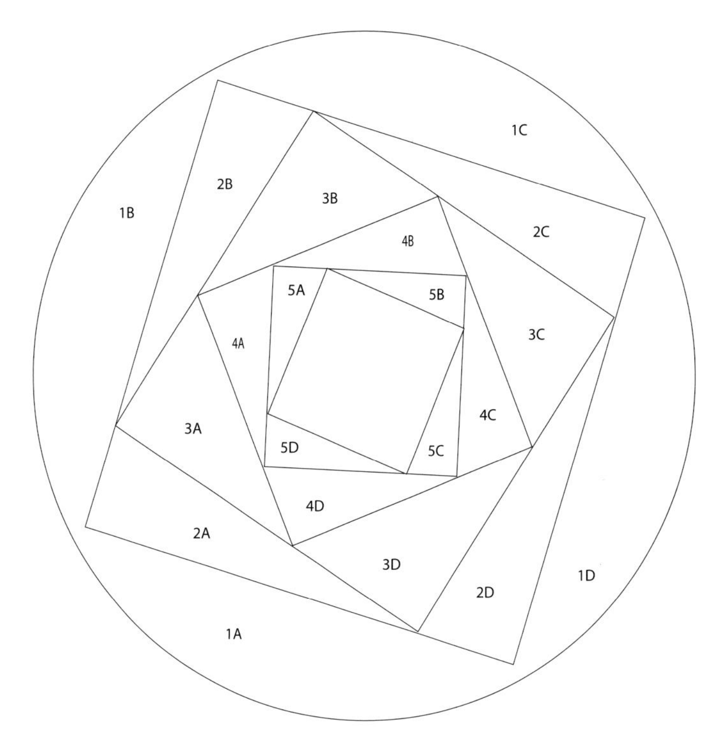

SIMPLE POP-UP, page 74

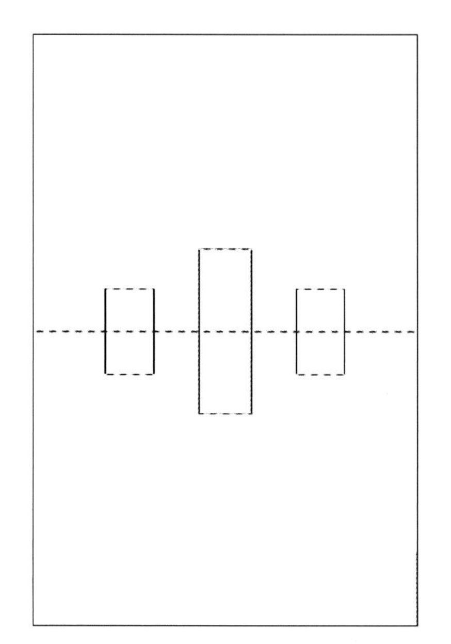

Cut on solid lines, fold on dotted lines.

PETAL FOLD, page 66

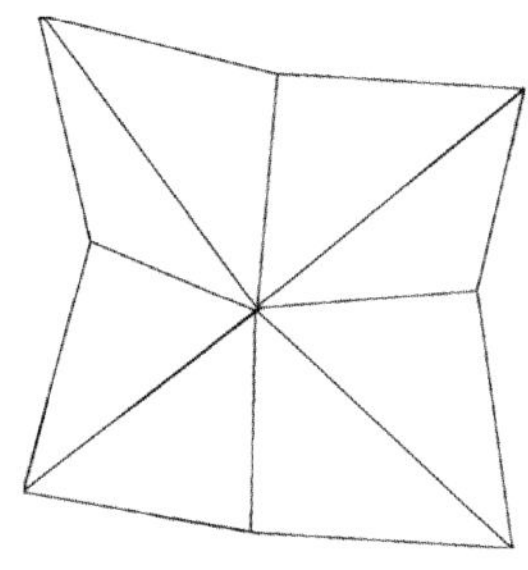

1. Fold and unfold a square in every direction.

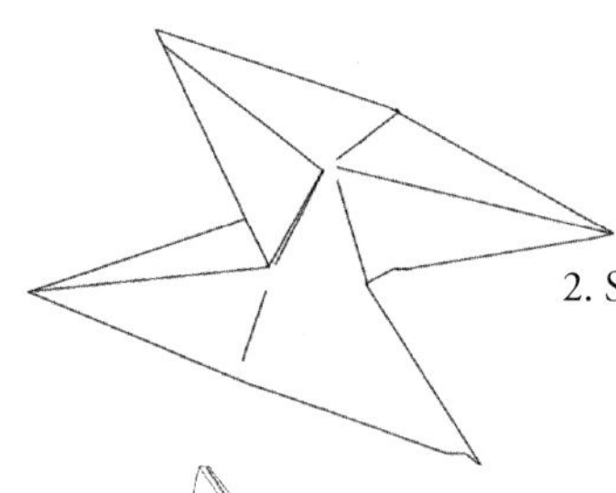

2. Squash in the sides.

3. You will now have a triangle.

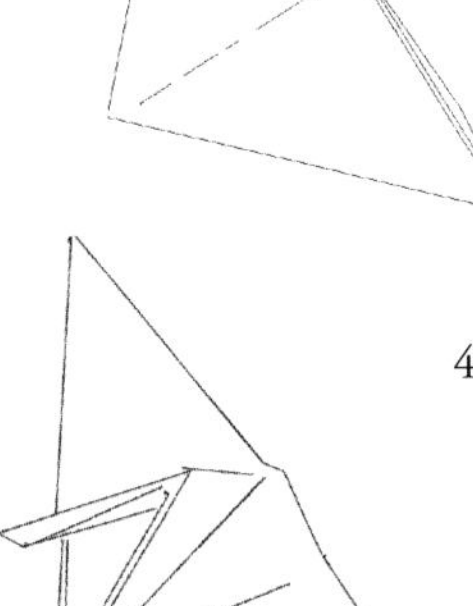

4. Bring 1 top layer forward and fold it down along the centerline to the tip of the triangle at the front.

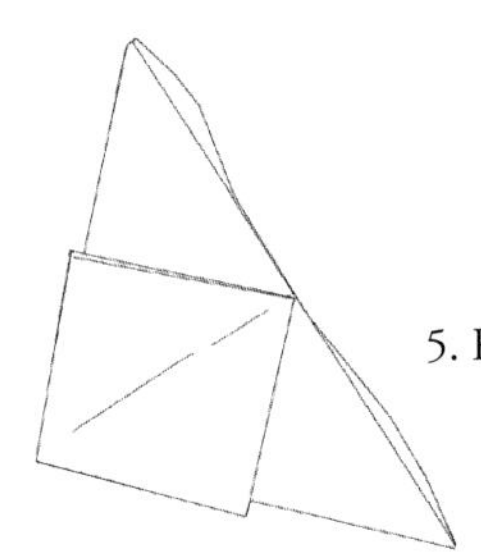

5. Repeat with the other top layer

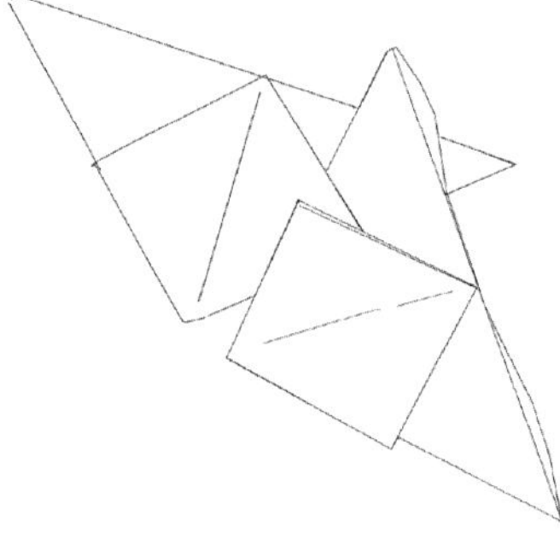

6. Tuck the separate triangles snugly under each other, each flap of the square under another.

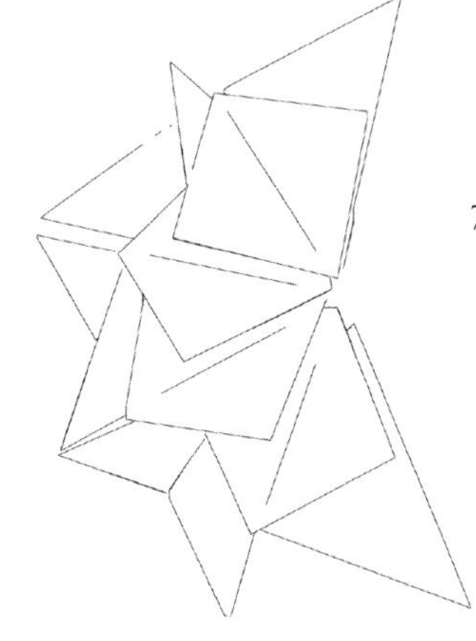

7. Make 6 Petal Folds. Assemble them in a circle with the points tightly together in the center. You can vary the arrangement by turning some triangles over.

DOUBLE KITE FOLD, page 43

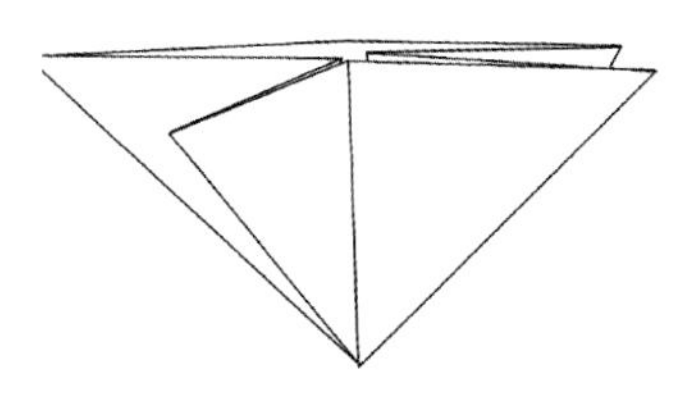

Follow steps 1-3 for PETAL FOLD on page 88.

4. Bring top right flap to center . . .

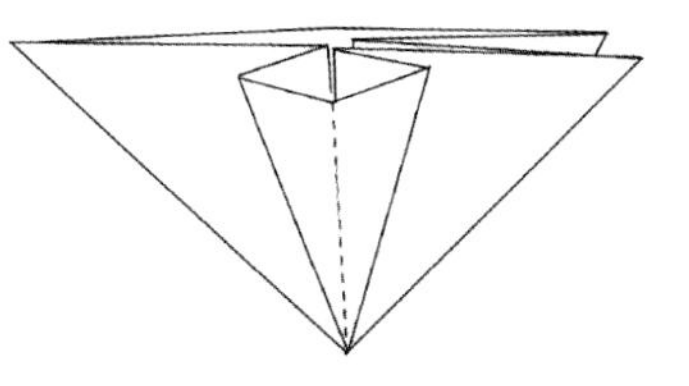

5. . . . and open the edges of the raised flap.

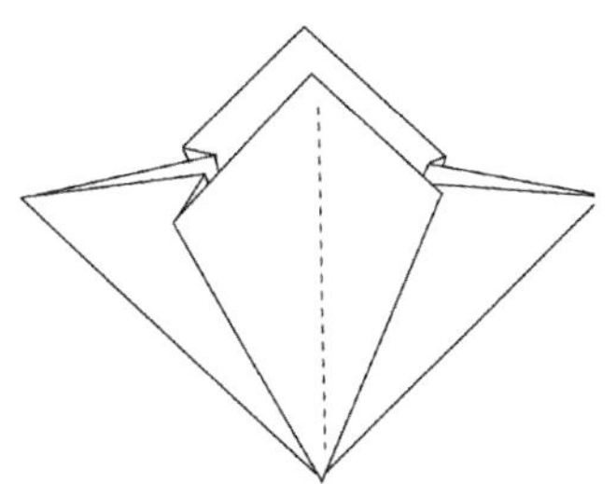

6. Press flat and crease both sides, keeping center creases aligned. Turn over and repeat steps with other flap.

4-FOLD WITH POCKETS, page 41

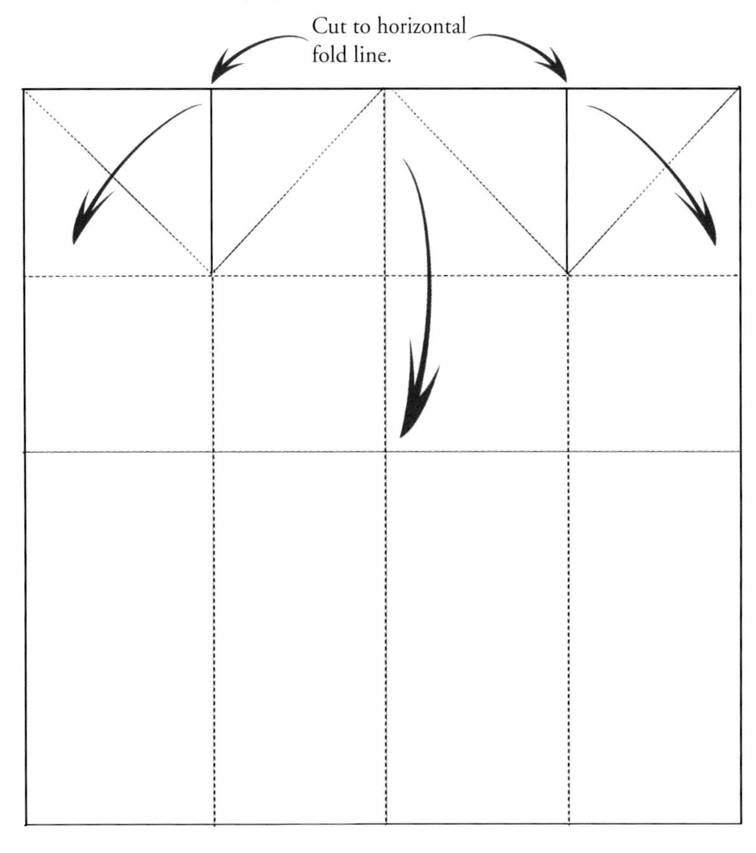

Fold diagonal lines. Mountain fold the horizontal line up behind.

FOLIO POCKET, page 34

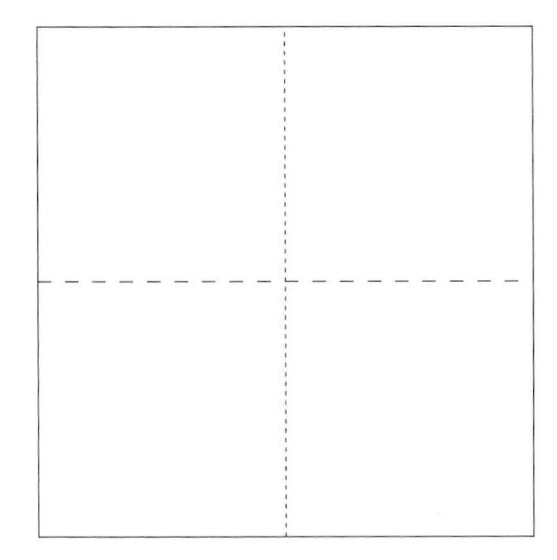

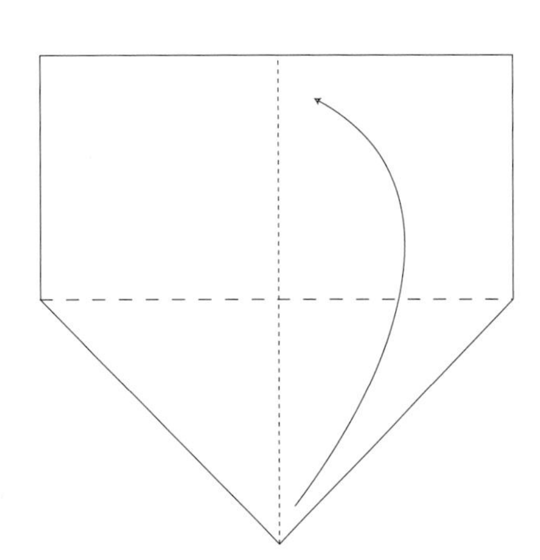

STAR SQUARE FOLD, page 35

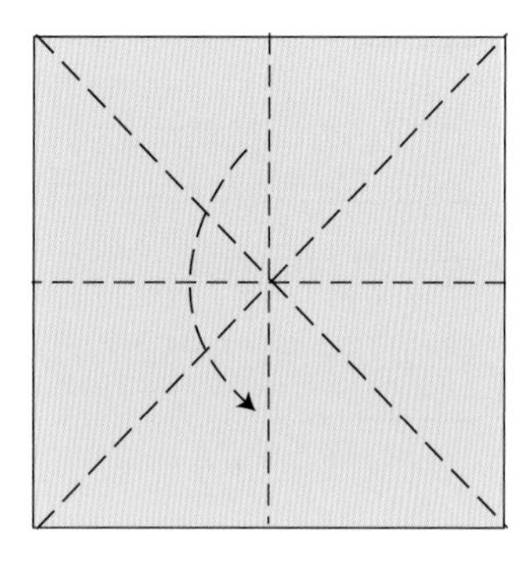

1. Fold a square of paper in half horizontally. Crease and unfold. Fold, crease and unfold. Fold in half diagonally both ways creasing and unfolding each time.

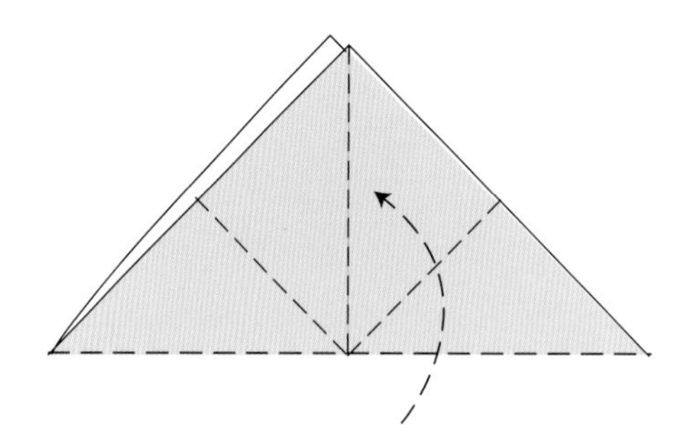

2. Turn paper with point up.

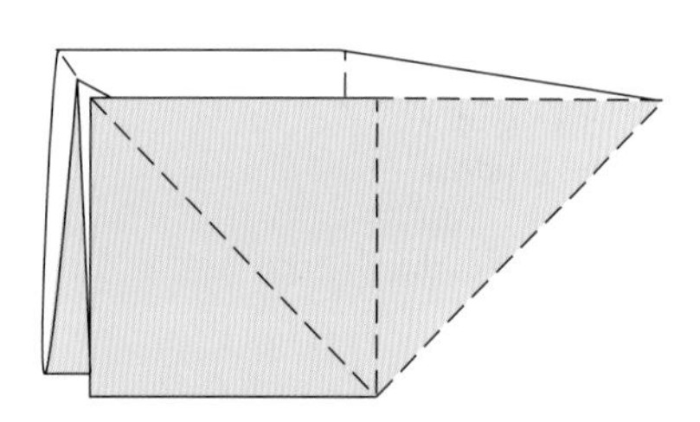

3. Squash the left triangletip up behnd the front square. Squash the right triangle tip behind the square.

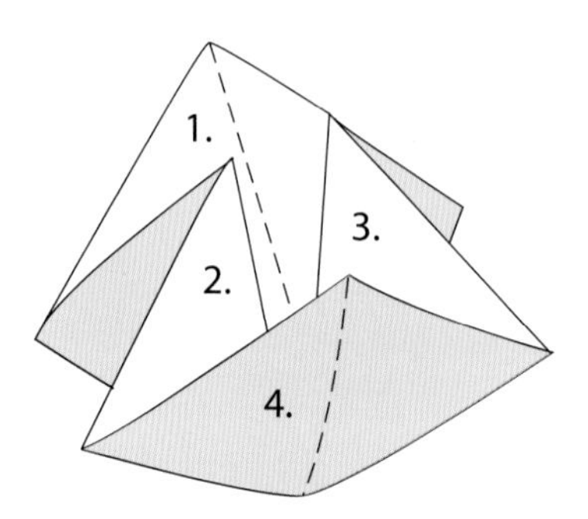

4. Flatten the square with point up and 2 layers on each side.

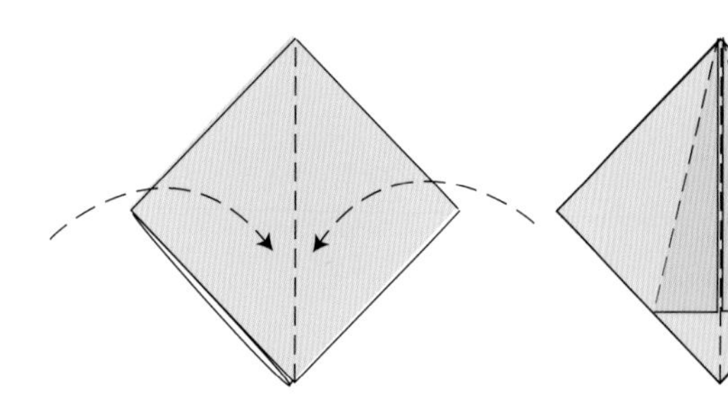

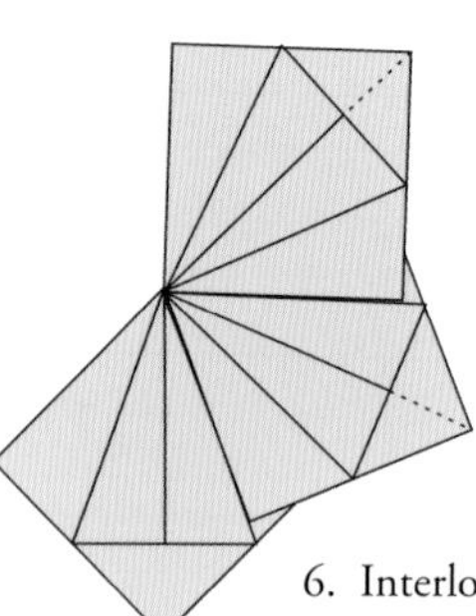

5. Fold the top layer on each side into the center.

6. Interlock: Slip the left point of the bottom layer of one piece under the top layer of another; repeat with al 8 folded diamonds. Dot glue in folds to secure.

FLOWER POT POP, page 54

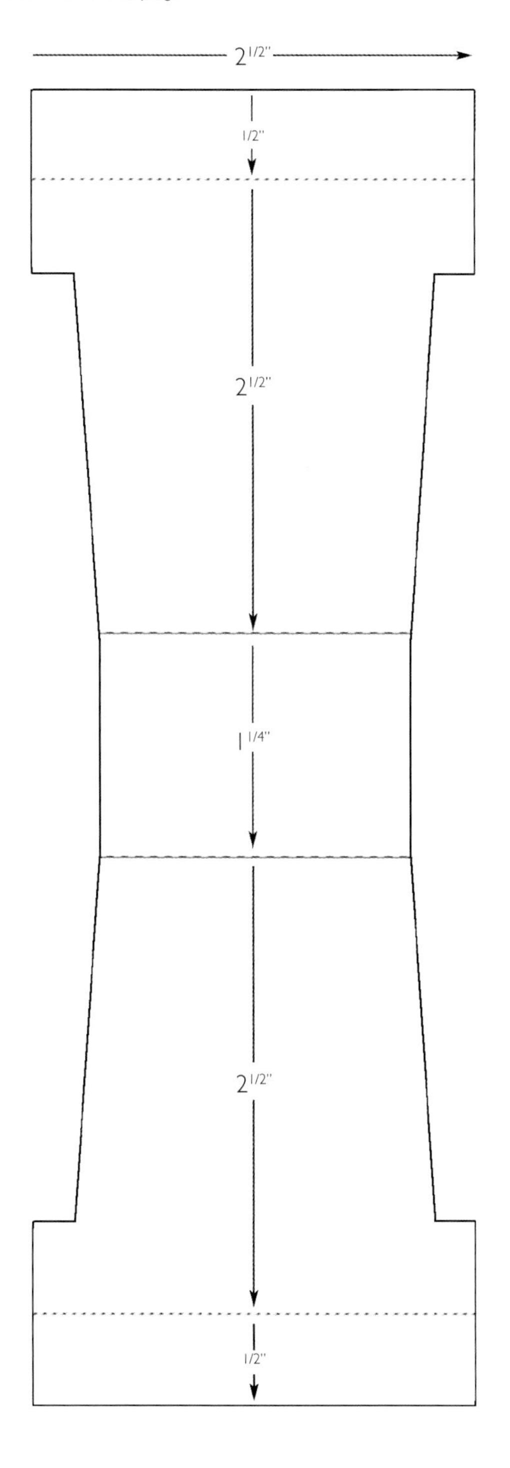

- Score where indicated.
- Fold the top edges in.
- Wrap the lollipop stick with ribbon.
- Tape the front and back sections together.
  (Lollipip is stabilized with a small piece of doube-sideed tape.)
- Attach the 2 rim pieces to the front and back.

QUILLING ROSES, page 66

Hold the quilling tool perpendicular in the right hand. Thread the quilling paper onto tool from the left side, with the paper horizontal to the tool. Roll the paper towards the left until you have made 1½ complete turns around the tool.

Making your first fold: With the left hand, fold the paper down towards your body. The quilling paper should now be perpendicular against the tool, both going in the same direction.

Hold the paper firmly in the left hand and rotate your right arm up while holding the tool. This should make the paper form a "cone" shape on the end of the tool. Bring your right arm back down making sure to keep the "cone" shape. For the rest of the folds: Repeat the same instructions used for the first fold until you are at the end of your strip of paper. Generally 3inches of paper will yield 7-9 folds.

Final forming of rose: Remove your folded rose from the tool. Using a pair of pointed tweezers, hold the very center of the rose & gently turn the paper outward, the opposite way you originally folded the paper. This opens up the rose slightly. Gently fold the petals of the rose

down by grabbing several layers of folds with the tweezers and pulling them down away from the center of the rose. The "crushed" look actually does come from gently "smashing" the rose between two fingers before gluing it into place.

OWL, page 61

OCTOPUS, page 61

MOUSE, page 61

Illustrated Glossary

ACCORDION FOLDING is a succession of alternating mountain and valley folds across the surface of a card, tag, or other paper surface. You can make small booklets or decorative embellishments with an extended series of accordion folds. See page 30.

COLLAGE is a collection of artfully arranged images, papers, or other materials pasted together on a page or paper-covered object. See page 80.

CUT-PAPER ARTWORK is a technique of cutting and layering small pieces of paper or the card or tag itself to create images with color, texture, and depth. See page 61.

EMBOSSING, INK Ink embossing is the process of raising a rubber-stamped image on paper by applying a special powder which, when heated, rises up and becomes permanent. See page 22

GATE FOLDING places the opening of a card at the center so that you can open both sides, like a gate, to reveal the interior. See page 43.

IRIS FOLDING involves arranging small cut strips of paper in a spiral pattern around a central opening, similar to the iris of the eye or lens of a camera. See page 42.

ORIGAMI is the traditional Japanese art of folding paper into representational shapes like these boxes. See page 30.

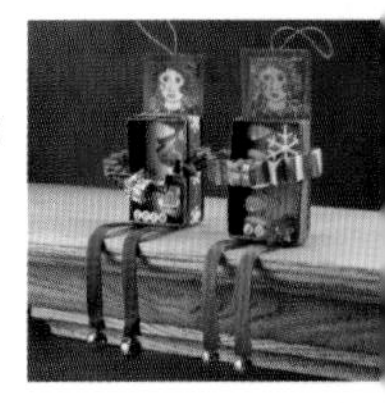

PAPER CONSTRUCTION involves building three-dimensional forms with paper and other embellishing materials. See page 79.

POP-UP CONSTRUCTION is the art of cutting, folding, and mounting an image on a card so that when you open the card the design literally pops up from the inside. See page 74.

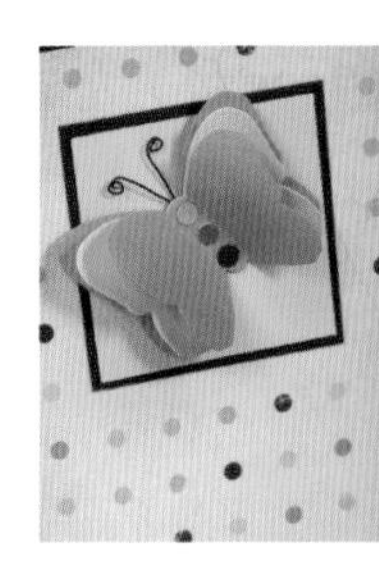

PAPER LAYERING can mean silhouetting an object and placing it on a design; placing light paper, like vellum, over an image to screen or soften the image; or framing an image by placing multiple papers behind it. See page 13.

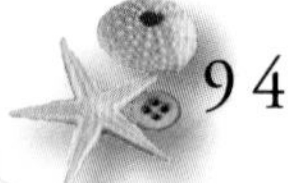

PUNCH ART is the process of cutting shapes from paper with a hand-held punch and either using the shapes alone or combining several shapes to create new, dimensional images. Both the positive and negative shapes can be useful. See page 52.

QUILLING, also called paper filigree or scroll work, is a simple decorative technique accomplished by rolling thin strips of paper around a slotted or needle tool into various shapes and then arranging and combining the shapes to embellish a design. See page 66.

RUBBER STAMPING is the technique of creating a design by tapping an inked rubber stamp on paper. The supplies you need for stamping are few: stamps, ink, paper. The supplies available for embellishing rubber stamping are many. See page 17.

SQUASHED TISSUE PAPER FLOWERS are created by accordion folding a stack of small pieces of issue paper, wrapping floral wire around the middle, and fanning out the paper, pinching each layer up toward the center.

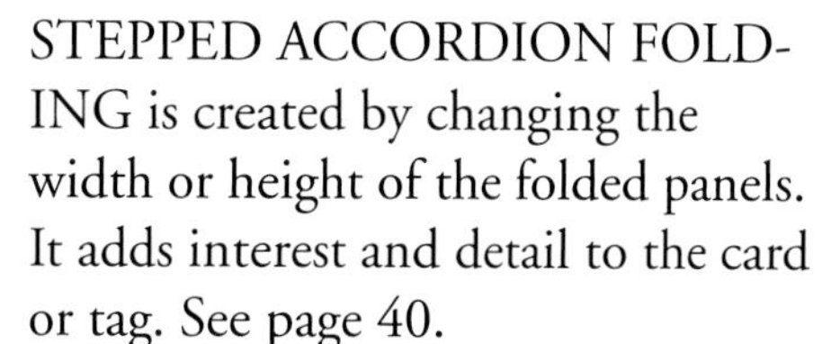

STEPPED ACCORDION FOLDING is created by changing the width or height of the folded panels. It adds interest and detail to the card or tag. See page 40.

TEA-BAG FOLDING, similar to origami, is the technique of folding small squares of usually printed paper into interesting geometric shapes that are artfully arranged in a pleasing pattern. It is sometimes called kaleidoscope folding. See page 36.

WINDOW CARDS are created by cutting appropriate-sized openings in one or more panels of a folded card, to reveal artwork visible through the cut opening. We have added a step to line the front of the card with an element hung between the two panels. See page 49.

ZENTANGLE is a process of drawing repeated doodling, usually with a fine black marker. The focused doodling is meant to relax and inspire creativity. See page 12.

Creative Techniques Papers